NINA BAROUGH

walking
for fitness

The low-impact
workout that tones
and shapes

LONDON, NEW YORK, MELBOURNE, MUNICH and DELHI

To all those who put their trust in me and Walked the Walk

Project Editor Jennifer Lane
Art Editor Ruth Hope
Senior Editor Jennifer Jones
Managing Editor Gillian Roberts
Managing Art Editor Karen Sawyer
Art Director Carole Ash
Category Publisher Mary-Clare Jerram
DTP Designer Sonia Charbonnier
Production Controller Rita Sinha
Photographer Russell Sadur

First published in the Great Britain in 2003
by Dorling Kindersley Ltd
80 Strand, London WC2R 0RL
Penguin Group (UK)

Every effort has been made to ensure that the information
in this book is accurate. However, neither the publisher nor
the author are engaged in rendering professional advice or
services to the individual reader. Always consult your doctor
before starting a fitness and/or nutrition programme if you
have any health concerns.

A CIP catalogue record for this book is
available from the British Library.

ISBN 1 4053 0092 2

Colour reproduced in Singapore
by Colourscan
Printed and bound in Portugal
by Printer Portuguesa

Discover more at
www.dk.com

CONTENTS

6   AUTHOR'S FOREWORD

8   THE POWER OF WALKING
10   What is power walking?
12   Why power walk?

16   GETTING STARTED
18   The right shoes for you
24   What to wear
28   Basic equipment

30   START WALKING
32   How fit are you?
36   Setting your stride
38   Planning your route
40   Posture and breathing
42   Power legs and feet
44   Power arms
46   Putting it all together
48   Common mistakes

50   STRETCH AND STRENGTHEN
52   Why stretch and strengthen?
60   Upper body stretches
64   Lower body stretches
66   Full body stretches
68   Before and after walking
72   Warm up and cool down
73   Stretch and strengthen plan

74   INNER STRENGTH, OUTER POWER
76   The power of breath
78   Think positive
80   Meeting the challenge
82   Meditate on your feet
84   Water
86   Healthy eating
88   Vitamins and minerals
90   Foods for fitness

92   WALKING FOR YOU
94   Fit walking into your day
96   One, two, three or more
98   Walking to lose weight
100   Walking and pregnancy
102   Walking with children
104   Walking for charities
106   Competitive walking

108   OUT AND ABOUT
110   Road walking
112   Trail walking
114   Walking in different climates
116   Safety

118   CARING FOR YOUR BODY
120   Be body aware
122   Pedicure
124   Massage your feet
126   Staying injury-free

132   TRAINING PROGRAMMES
134   Cross training
140   Beginner
142   Intermediate
144   Advanced
146   Short distance
148   Half marathon
150   Marathon
152   Weight loss

154   Useful resources
156   Index
158   Walking log
160   Acknowledgments

AUTHOR'S FOREWORD

This is a book about discovering how to power walk and the astounding number of benefits that come with it. It is about not only learning how our bodies work, but also realizing that our attitudes and beliefs, what we eat and drink, and even how we breathe all create who we are. You will find out how small and simple changes can ultimately have a huge impact on your health, fitness, and quality of life.

In 1997 I discovered I had breast cancer. My world fell apart, and all the beliefs and ideals that I had held for so many years were suddenly challenged and put to the absolute test. I am not sure whether I supported the charity Walk the Walk I had started only months earlier or it supported me, but what I do know is that I became totally focused on my health and this is when the wonders of power walking really became apparent to me.

During my months of treatment, I used power walking, diet, vitamins, positive thinking, and visualization to help manage and conquer my cancer, and as a result I became fitter, had more energy, and felt more vibrant and balanced than at any other time in my life.

For me, walking is magical. After a few minutes I start to feel my shoulders relax, my chest open, my breath begins to deepen and my lungs fill with air. Best of all, I feel as though I have shaken off a heavy cloak and the day's activities fall away from me. After 30 minutes of powerful walking nothing ever seems that big or bad, and I feel great. It is my biggest wish that this book will not only encourage you to step out of your door and start walking, but inspire you to look at all aspects of your life.

Enjoy your walking!

THE POWER OF WALKING

We all have dreams of becoming fitter, leaner, and stronger, and bursting with health and energy. Power walking can bring you all these benefits. The technique provides a simple yet effective way of giving your whole body a thorough workout. You may also discover, as many others have, that power walking opens you to new experiences and that it brings mental well-being as well as physical health.

"Twenty years from now you will be more disappointed by the things you didn't do than by the ones you did. So throw off the bowlines, sail away from the safe harbor. Catch the trade winds in your sails. Explore. Dream. Discover." MARK TWAIN

WHAT IS POWER WALKING?

Walking is the most natural and fundamental of all human conscious movements; by putting one foot in front of the other and moving your arms in opposition, you can propel yourself forward at approximately 5km/h (3mph). Add the "power", change your focus, adjust your technique, and the pace can increase to 8km/h (5mph) or more. All the muscles in your body are used to create a dynamic aerobic activity that helps you to achieve optimum well-being and fitness.

Many people take up walking as a hobby or for the sake of fitness because it is so accessible. It is a low-impact form of exercise because it does not put undue stress and strain on your joints. This means it carries a low risk of injury. You also don't need to go through the pain threshold as you do with some other sports; it is up to you to choose how challenging you want it to be.

Categories of walking

There are five main walking styles, though they come with a confusing variety of titles – for example, athletic walking, fitness walking, and dynamic walking are all names used for power walking. However, the five categories are quite clearly defined by speed and technique.

The stroll This is a casual pace, slower than the average walk. A person strolling would find it takes around 20 minutes or more to walk a kilometre (30 minutes or more to walk a mile).

THE POPULAR CHOICE

Walking used to be considered an easy option in exercise, or as nothing more than a way of getting from A to B. Walking for health and fitness is now a highly popular sport for all ages, with millions of people taking part worldwide, on their own or in groups. Power or fitness walking has gained such popularity that it is now a more common route to fitness than running.

The average walk Everyone has their own walking speed in everyday life, but the average is considered to be approximately 5km/h (3mph). This would mean an average walker would take 12 minutes to walk a kilometre (20 minutes to walk a mile), though most people probably could not sustain this speed for more than an hour or so.

Power walking The stroll and the average walk are defined simply by speed because technique is not much of a consideration. You will naturally swing your arms in opposition to your legs to aid your balance and to help you to move forward. However, with the next pace, power walking, the technique is specific and important.

A power walker can reach speeds of up to 8km/h (5mph), which means walking a kilometre in less than 8 minutes (a mile in 12 minutes). To propel forwards, a power walker pushes off each stride from the toes with a straight back leg for extra strength and stability. This is where the power comes from and why the push off is so important. The arm movement is also vital to a power walker's speed and drive, with both elbows at a 90 degree angle, the arms punching back and forth in a piston-like action. Turn to pp42–49 to read about the exact technique.

Speed walking This is the next category as you step up your exertion a gear from power walking. The pace of a speed walker is in excess of 8km/h (5mph). A useful description of speed walking is to think that it is in relation to racewalking as jogging

is to running. A power walker who continually works at his or her speed will eventually reach this category naturally.

Racewalking Also known as Olympic walking, this is the ultimate pace with regard to speed. Racewalkers reach speeds of 14.5km/h (9mph) or more, and are mainly concerned with speed and competing (*see pp106–107 for more information on the rules*). They have their own technique and strict rules and move with the familiar hip-roll and wiggle that many people think of when power walking is mentioned. The technique used for power walking is a simplified forerunner of racewalking.

Perfecting the pace

The beauty of power walking is that you can progress from being an average walker to a power walker in a matter of weeks. Putting in the extra effort to begin power walking, rather than just

Power walkers always give the impression that they are striding out with great purpose and determination, which they most probably are.

strolling, means that your heart rate will be raised to a higher level. Working the heart in this way is what makes power walking a cardiovascular aerobic activity that is perfect to keep you fit and healthy (*see pp34–35*). Power walking can burn the same number of calories as does running. Many people want the health benefits and physical exertion that running achieves, but don't want to put such a strain on their bodies. Power walking fits this exact specification.

The benefits of power walking (*see pp12–15*) have led to it becoming a mainstream and extremely popular sport in many countries. It is the most natural form of exercise, it requires very little equipment, yet it offers so many benefits.

WHY POWER WALK?

Researchers in the field of sports and fitness have described walking as "the nearest activity to perfect exercise". It seems far too simple to claim that a basic skill that most of us do without a second thought can be so significant, but as you begin to learn more about your body and the benefits of walking you will realize that it is true; the action of walking may be simple but the results for your health and daily living are far-reaching.

Our society is becoming more and more sedentary and overweight. We sit in our cars instead of walking, many of us spend hours seated at a desk at work, and thanks to computers we can now do a lot of our shopping without leaving home. Not surprisingly, more and more people complain of posture-related aches and pains, and life really is no fun if every day is a battle to find our energy and sparkle. Yet we are missing one vital point. Exercise in any shape or form is an essential part of our lives, not an optional extra that we may or may not choose to do.

Making the commitment

Exercise is often seen as something undertaken to get rid of a beer belly, or to fit back into a smaller dress size, particularly in the summer months. You don't often hear people say that they must do some exercise to clear their mind, or to make them feel happy. Yet in truth, the health of your mind, body and spirit are all inextricably linked. Imagine yourself as a triangle, supported in each corner. If one support goes, the others are put under tremendous strain to keep you balanced. That challenge is continually happening in our bodies, but walking can help to keep that balance.

Walking alone or in company is the best exercise you can do for strengthened muscles, a healthy heart, a toned body, and a clear, focused mind.

Committing yourself to exercise can be very like dieting; the desire to do it comes and goes in phases. We have all been there. We know we should do it, but we need to be in the right frame of mind. We then get enthusiastic and eager to transform ourselves. We go to the gym or follow a programme for weeks or maybe months, feel great and vow to keep it up. However, for some reason we break the routine, and then suddenly we are back at square one, thinking we must get fit.

This is familiar cycle to most people, and just like on-off dieting, it doesn't work. To change this pattern the first thing you must do is to ask the question, "Why hasn't it worked?" The answer is usually boredom, and not achieving the results and quick fix that you want. A major key to finding a lifelong sport that you can stick at is choosing something that is fun, motivational, has variety, can be as challenging as you want it to be, achieves physical results, suits your body, and fits easily in to your life. Keeping active is commonsense body maintenance that will ensure you can still choose to power walk and enjoy life to the full when you are well into your eighties and beyond.

Take a step in the right direction

Just by taking that first step towards power walking, you will be considering your walking posture and helping your back to become stronger and more flexible. Walking is also an aerobic exercise, which means it pumps blood to your muscles to be used as energy. Because walking requires the use of your arms, legs, torso, and many muscle groups, any amount of regular walking will increase your cardiovascular strength. This in turn will increase your ability to do more without getting tired. By being able to do more you will also be building muscular endurance, which means you will keep going longer with sustained energy. Imagine flying through all your daily chores and still having the energy to go out and walk a few miles.

THE BENEFITS OF POWER WALKING

• Reduces tension, stress, and anxiety, and enhances mental well-being.

• Tones and strengthens your muscles.

• Improves muscular endurance and flexibility.

• Helps manage body weight and reduce body fat.

• Boosts your immune system.

• Relieves the symptoms of premenstrual tension.

• Increases bone strength and prevents osteoporosis.

• Reduces the risk of cancers.

• Improves cardiovascular fitness which can help reduce the risk of coronary disease and strokes.

• Is socially enjoyable.

• Detoxes the body and improves skin texture.

• Improves sleep patterns.

• Eases the pain and stiffness of arthritis.

• Reduces the risk of Type 2 diabetes.

• Boosts the level of HDL (healthy cholesterol) in the blood and reduces high blood pressure.

• Helps you stop smoking and promotes healthy eating.

• Improves energy levels and self-esteem.

• Relieves and prevents back pain.

Although walking does not exercise all your muscles, it does work hard on the back of your body, in particular your calves, hamstrings, gluteals, upper body back muscles and shoulders. Because your other muscles need to keep flexible and working too, I have included in this book some daily stretching exercises and other activities to complement your walking so that you will use your body to its full capacity.

Preventing ill health

The impact of weight on your bones and joints as you walk will strengthen them and ultimately protect them against osteoporosis. Although this disease is more common with older people, when their bones become weak and can be prone to fractures, it is never too late or early to build bone density.

Walking will also increase your circulation and speed up your metabolism, which not only means that you will burn more calories but your body will become more efficient at absorbing the nutrients from your food. In turn this will encourage you to drink more water. Insufficient intake of water is the source of many disorders. Drinking more can help to improve your digestion and detoxify and cleanse your system. Among other benefits, this will give you a more efficiently working body and radiant skin.

It may be hard to imagine but it is nevertheless true that walking for 30 minutes a day will bring huge benefits for your immune system. The stronger your immune system is, the more protection against ill health you will consequently have. It is your barrier against absolutely everything that your body has to confront on a day-to-day basis, from the common cold, flu, pollution and stress to heart disease and cancers, so it is important that you keep it functioning to its optimum level.

The mind-body connection

If you are aware of your body at all, you will know how tired and sluggish you become both physically and mentally if you go through periods of inactivity. Untroubled, natural sleep can often be so elusive. One of the major benefits of power walking that you will notice very quickly is how soundly you sleep. We all need different amounts, but having enough sleep can make you feel calmer, more in control, more tolerant and patient, more enthusiastic about trying new things and challenges, more joyful and content. Restful sleep can be the magic key to the quality of your life.

Stress is another drain on our resources and can lead to all sorts of complaints from asthma and high blood pressure to depression and anxiety. Walking has been shown to be a positive way of relieving stress and improving self-esteem. It gives you the space to think, solve problems and gain clarity. Walking in parks or anywhere that feels close to nature will also bring a sense of peace in difficult times.

Premenstrual tension may be caused by a physical change, but the effect on mood is something that most women experience. However, walking and exercise can reduce the symptoms and keep your serenity intact.

Life is good

With a healthy body, plenty of sleep and a clear mind it would be difficult not to have a spring in your step and to feel that life is good. Exercise releases endorphins often called "happy hormones", which is why you always feel so good after you have been active. Combine that with walking with friends or family and you will have an enriched spirit. Alternatively, if you want to expand your creativity, walk alone and let the energy of nature inspire you.

As your health and fitness levels increase, you will begin to see the excitement in life's challenges. Perhaps these include losing weight, or maybe you will decide to take part in a marathon. The possibilities are different for everyone, but what is the same is that we all need the necessary vitality, to be excited by them and to visualize our dreams coming true. I have been able to witness and share enriching experiences with many women and men who originally decided to start power walking just to get fit. Believe me, there is nothing quite as exciting as witnessing flowers bloom.

GETTING STARTED

You don't need to invest in special clothes or equipment to power walk effectively, but good shoes are essential and will ensure that you walk to the best of your ability. This is especially important when you consider that each time the foot strikes the ground it bears two-and-a-quarter times the body's weight, and that it is estimated that a relatively active person will take 8,000–10,000 steps a day, and walk 83,000 miles in a lifetime.

(The foot is) "a masterpiece of engineering and a work of art." LEONARDO DA VINCI

THE RIGHT SHOES FOR YOU

Our feet are one of the most complex parts of the body. Each foot is made up of 26 bones, 32 joints, hundreds of nerve endings, and four layers of muscle that fit between the sole and the top of the foot. In addition, feet come in all shapes and sizes. If we want our feet to perform well, we need to make sure that they have the right footwear to do the job.

How you walk

Most feet fall into one of three walking styles: those that pronate, those that supinate, and those that are neutral. It is important that you know which category you fit into when you buy shoes, as some have insoles built in to correct excessive pronation or supination. To determine what kind of foot you have, try the following wet foot test.

Footprint analysis

Dip your foot in water, shake off most of the excess, and then walk across a large sheet of card, or a dark-tiled floor if you have one.

If you leave a footprint that forms a flat, solid band, with little or no distinction where the arch should be, then you are a pronator. A low arch, or flat feet, can exacerbate this. This is the most common bearing, and while a certain amount of pronation, where the foot rolls inwards and the arches flatten, is normal, with excessive pronation (also known as overpronation) there is a pronounced inward roll of the foot as it lands. This can twist the foot, shin, knee, and hip, and can cause stress throughout the body. Other symptoms of excessive pronation are rough skin forming on the inside edge of the foot (the medial) and on the heel.

TREAD WEAR

The soles of an existing pair of your shoes will also reveal your walking gait. Place the heels together so that you can see them at eye level. If the heels are worn on the inside and the shoes lean in then you pronate. If the heels are worn on the outside and the shoes lean out you supinate. If they are not excessively worn on either side your walking gait is neutral.

Pronation (left foot) | tread worn on inside **Neutral** (left foot) | tread worn evenly **Supination** (left foot) | tread worn outside

If you leave a footprint that shows just the toes, ball of your foot, and heel, then you are a supinator. Supination (also called underpronation) is where the feet do not have enough inward motion, and roll to the outside edge of the foot after landing. As a result, hard skin may form on the outside edge of the foot.

If your footprint is somewhere in between the two, then your feet are neutral (pronation neutral). Here, the foot neither excessively pronates nor supinates, and the centre of the heel strikes the ground. The soles of your shoes will also reveal a great deal about the way you walk – study the diagrams opposite to learn more about tread wear.

Causes and cures

There are many causes of excessive pronation and supination, including corns, bunions, and other foot complaints, knee problems, or being overweight. Walking at even a few degrees out from the neutral gait can cause your body to overcompensate and take it out of alignment. To correct excessive pronation, look for a shoe that will support the inside edge of your foot, and has extra stability in the heel. If you are a supinator, ideally you should have a shoe that has good heel stability and extra cushioning under the ball of the foot. If you have a neutral gait, you can wear any good-quality shoe.

It is also possible to self-treat minor pronation and, to a lesser degree, supination by using ready-made corrective insoles, or orthotics. These are designed to support your foot in the necessary places to correct your gait and prevent injury. However, if in doubt, do not attempt to diagnose the problem yourself, but seek advice from a properly qualified chiropodist or podiatrist (foot specialists) and get a professional bio-mechanical assessment of your feet. A foot specialist will also arrange for bespoke orthotics to be made up for you.

KEY POINTS TO LOOK FOR

• Which is your bigger foot? It is common to have one foot bigger than the other. Buy shoes that fit your bigger foot, and make adjustments to the fit of the smaller foot with insoles.

• Which is your longest toe? Usually, this is the big toe, but sometimes the second toe is the longest. There should be a two-finger width between the end of your longest toe and the end of the shoe (see p20).

• Are your feet wide or narrow? Most shoes come in one width, and while the fit can be adjusted slightly by the way that you lace your shoes (see pp22–23), if you have very wide or narrow feet you will need to buy shoes that are sold in different width sizes (see Resources p154–155).

• Do you have a slim heel? This is a common feature in women, and may be combined with a wide fitting across the broadest part of the foot. Lacing your shoe to accommodate a narrow heel may help (see p23).

• Do you have large toe joints or bunions? If you do, you may want to see a podiatrist for expert advice on shoe fit.

Shoes for walking

Many people ask the question, "Can I wear a running shoe for power walking?" Well, you wouldn't expect to perform well if you played tennis in football boots, and the same applies to walking and running shoes. A shoe suitable for power walking must be flexible; at push off, a power walker's forefoot flexes at nearly twice the angle of a runner's. The shoe needs to be pliable enough to follow the roll of the foot as you lead the heel-to-toe action. A walker lands on the heel, so good supportive cushioning in the heel is essential. The height of the heel on a walking shoe also needs to be on the low side. Many running shoes have quite a high heel, which when you power walk can force you to overwork the shin muscles and cause injury.

If you are unable to find a walking shoe, a running shoe is your next best choice. However, try to find a shoe that has as many of the key points that you are looking for as possible (*see opposite*). Avoid cross trainers as the soles are usually too rigid for power walking.

Shopping for shoes

Choose a specialist athletics shoe shop that has a good reputation and trained staff. The staff should be able to assess your feet and direct you towards a selection of shoes that are right for you. The best shops have a treadmill so that you can try the shoes in action; some shops will even allow you to take a quick "test walk" outside on the pavement.

Buy shoes in the afternoon. Feet swell slightly throughout the day and when you walk vigorously, so always try on shoes when your feet are at their largest. Take with you a list of your feet details (*see p19*) so that you don't forget any important points about fit. Also make a note of any injuries past and present. They may have a bearing on which shoe you choose. Study the page opposite and note the key features you should be looking for in your walking shoes. Take your walking socks with you. You should always match your walking socks to your shoes so that they work together. Also take along your orthotics if you wear them. Finally, remember that shoes come in all price ranges, but expensive does not necessarily mean the best for you.

ORTHOTICS

These corrective insoles are designed to change the motion of the foot, in particular to relieve excessive pronation, and to stop further deterioration of the foot for those with flat feet or bunions. Preformed orthotics are available on the high street, while bespoke orthotics are made after a bio-mechanical assessment of your foot by a qualified podiatrist or chiropodist. They are designed specifically for your feet, and may include features such as heel lifts.

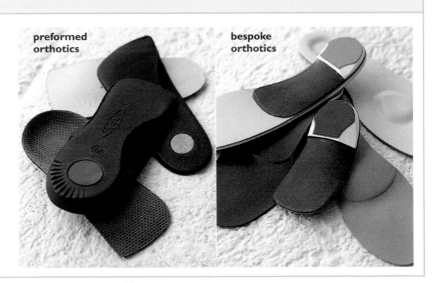

preformed orthotics

bespoke orthotics

WHAT TO LOOK FOR

A shoe suitable for power walking must be light and flexible so that it can mimic the range of movement from the foot. Make sure that the toe box is roomy and rounded so that your toes can move freely; unless you have very slender feet, avoid tapered toe boxes. You will need to have at least a two-finger width between your longest toe and the end of the shoe to allow sufficient space for the push-off movement.

Low-cut heel
This prevents cutting into the Achilles tendon. Must be cushioned so that the heel does not slide as you push off.

Lightweight
Do not carry any more weight than you need to.

Flexibility A good walking shoe should be flexible while protective, allowing the foot to have a full range of movement from heel to toe.

Toe box
This needs to be roomy, deep, and preferably rounded so that your toes have plenty of room to spread and are protected at "push off".

Low heel profile
Make sure that the heel of the shoe is low.

Arch support
There should be good arch support and insole.

Cushioning
Supportive cushioning is essential, especially in the heel and under the ball of the foot.

When you are trying on a pair of shoes, your feet should feel well supported and protected inside the shoes, comfortable and without any pressure on any part of your feet, held well in the heels, and supported under the arches. It is worth noting that walking shoes, as with most sports shoes, tend to be small for their size, and you will probably need to try on shoes that are anything between one and two sizes larger than you normally wear.

Pay particular attention to the toe box. Some toe boxes can be quite tapered, and unless you have very slender feet your toes can bunch up slightly. This may feel fine in the shop, but as soon as you start to walk any distance your toes will start to rub against the shoe, causing blisters and bruising. Make sure, too, that there is a two-finger width between your longest toe and the end of your shoe.

You should not have to "wear in" shoes. If they pinch or rub in the slightest way leave them on the shelf. You want to walk out of the shop ready to go a million miles.

Caring for your shoes

Now that you have the perfect shoes, help them to last. If you get your shoes wet, remove the insoles and dry them separately. Stuff the shoes with

---

LACING TECHNIQUES

The way that you lace your shoes can further improve the fit of your shoes. This is especially useful if, for example, you have a wide foot but a narrow heel.

Always loosen your laces before you slip into the shoes to prevent stress on the eyelets and wear on the heels of the shoes. Tighten your laces from the bottom eyelets, closest to your toes, to the top of the shoe, pulling the laces tight at each set of eyelets before going on to the next set.

The standard crisscross lacing suits most people, and allows you to tighten the laces more evenly than bar lacing. Most shoes have double eyelets at the top. Use them both for a firm fit for a slim foot, or leave the top set unlaced if you have a high instep or a broad foot.

Lacing for a wide foot
To give you extra width across the foot, thread the laces through the bottom two loops or holes as usual. Miss out the next two loops by threading the laces up the side of the shoe. In the middle of the shoe start to lace crisscross again to the top of the shoe.

Lacing for a narrow foot
Lace the first two sets of eyelets as normal. Keeping the laces on the side of their last eyelet, thread to the next hole. Cross the laces over and thread them back through the bar that has been created on each side, pulling in tight. Resume threading crisscross as normal to the top of the shoe.

newspaper to absorb the moisture, and dry them slowly away from direct heat. Remove the paper after a few hours once it has soaked up as much moisture as possible. Don't try to hurry the drying process by putting wet shoes on or near a heat source, such as radiator, as this will make the materials in the shoe crack and weaken. Do not put your shoes into the washing machine to clean them. Again, this will speed the break-down of materials in the shoe. Wipe off any dirt with a damp cloth and leave them to air. If your shoes are very muddy, lightly scrub off the mud under lukewarm running water. Then dry them as before.

Don't store your shoes in a plastic bag or box. Leave them out to air between wearings. If possible, buy two pairs of shoes so that you can rotate their use.

Replace your shoes every 800–1125km (500–700 miles); write the date of purchase inside the shoe so you don't forget. After this amount of wear they may still look good on the outside, but they will have deteriorated on the inside to the point where they no longer support your foot properly. My shoes usually let me know when they need changing. A really comfortable pair of shoes will suddenly start to give me blisters, or pain in my ankles as the support slackens.

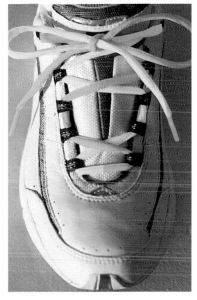

Lacing for a wide or deep arch
Start to lace as normal with the first two sets of eyelets. Miss out the next two eyelets in the middle of the shoe, threading the laces up the side of the shoe. Then continue lacing as normal to the top of the shoe.

Lacing for a narrow or slipping heel
Lace your shoe as normal to the last but one set of eyelets. Make a bar on each side as in lacing for a narrow foot. Loop each lace across and through the bar and pull tight. Tie as normal.

FOR HIKING ONLY

I have seen people end up in a lot of pain when they try to power walk in hiking boots. The very features that make hiking boots ideal for carrying you great distances over rugged terrain – the rigid sole, and a firmly supported ankle – will cause major problems to your feet when power walking. Always wear the right shoes.

WHAT TO WEAR

Comfort and practicality are the key qualities you should look for when choosing clothes for power walking. The goal is to enjoy walking and to be totally unaware of what you are wearing – that's when you know your clothes are really working for you. If you are walking in extremely hot or cold weather, turn to pages 114–115 to find out more about what to wear in such conditions.

Legs and layers

After shoes, the next most important consideration is what to wear on your bottom half. Ideally, opt for leggings or shorts that are made from a synthetic, or synthetic mix, stretch fabric that breathes and wicks away moisture from your body to the outside of the fabric, where it evaporates. Make sure that they are not too tight around the waist, and check for minimal flat seams. Walkers move with a scissor-like action, so any garments that have thick inside seams, such as jog pants or jeans, will cause chaffing on the insides of the thighs and a great deal of discomfort.

A mistake that many people make when they start power walking is to wear too many clothes on their top halves. Your temperature can rise and fall quite dramatically throughout a walk, so the trick is to wear thin layers. Start with a vest or T-shirt, then add a lightweight sweatshirt or jacket (*see box, right*). If your second layer has long sleeves, you can tie it around your waist when you are not wearing it. Some manufacturers make jackets that fold into themselves to form a bum bag, complete with straps and buckle to fix around your waist, when they are not being worn.

When it comes to choosing fabrics, again select those made from synthetic materials, or a mixture of man-made and natural fibres, that allow the skin to breathe and will wick away sweat from the body. Cotton feels lovely to put on, but if you tend to sweat and become very hot, it will cling to you and become wet and cold. Always make sure you have a layer to put on at the end of your walk. If at all possible, wear light colours and garments that sport luminous strips so that if you are walking at dusk or in the dark you can be seen easily. (*For more information on walking and safety, see pp116–117.*)

The other helpful item of clothing is a baseball cap. Wear it to keep the sun out of your eyes when it's hot, and to retain heat when it's cold. Again, opt for a quick-drying man-made fabric over cotton.

OUT IN THE RAIN OR WIND

• When it is wet, you need a lightweight jacket in a man-made fabric such as Gore-tex that is water-resistant and allows your body to breathe inside the jacket. This is not the same as waterproof, which will rapidly turn your jacket into a sauna.

• Make sure that the jacket cuffs can be drawn tight to prevent water getting in, and that the back is long enough to cover your bottom and keep it dry. The neck of the jacket should be high enough to keep out drips, and a peaked hood will stop the rain from falling on your face.

• You may also want to wear gloves in a lightweight man-made fibre, depending on the severity of the rain and the time of year (see *also* pp114–115).

• If you are walking in strong winds, you need a jacket that has a drawstring bottom to keep the wind out. Again, the best fabric for a windproof jacket is a synthetic one, which will be both tough and light.

HIGH-PERFORMANCE WEAR

When the weather is warm, a vest top and stretch shorts are the ideal gear for power walking; add a long-sleeved garment tied around your waist to put on at the end of your walk so you don't cool down too quickly. In cooler weather, keep warm by wearing a long-sleeved T-shirt under a lightweight jacket and stretch leggings.

Baseball cap
Protects from sun in summer, and retains heat in winter.

Lightweight jacket
Sleeves are loose enough to allow the arms to swing.

Vest top
An excellent foundation item to which you can add further layers.

Sweatshirt
A light, long-sleeved garment provides a layer of warmth when needed.

Pale colours
These will attract attention at dawn, dusk, and night.

Shorts
Stretch shorts are comfortable, and won't rise up the insides of your legs.

Leggings
These should fit comfortably, with no raised seams.

A good foundation

All women, regardless of their breast size, should wear a sports bra – it is an essential piece of equipment. It is important not only to find a bra that suits you and feels comfortable, but also one that gives you proper support. The breasts are made of delicate tissue, not muscle. Vigorous movement may stretch or tear the tissue, and once it has been damaged, the tissue cannot repair itself, so a supportive bra is vital.

Make sure that your bra fits you correctly. It is estimated that 70 per cent of women are wearing the wrong size of bra, so if you are in doubt, get measured professionally. It is worth bearing in mind that regular exercise will almost definitely change your body shape over a period of time, and your bra size may change, too.

Some sports bras come with a guide as to the type of exercise for which they are most suited, that is gentle, moderate, or vigorous. I class power walking as moderate to vigorous exercise, depending on your goal. Bras made from synthetic, or a mixture of natural and synthetic, fibres are best as they have moisture-wicking properties and allow the skin to breathe. Some bras include a silver fibre, which is said to neutralize bacteria in the area. Others are designed to house a heart-rate monitor, a useful feature if you want to wear one.

Buy two sports bras so that having one in the wash does not stop you walking. Replace a sports bra within 6–12 months, especially if you are walking 3–4 times a week. Over time, it will lose its elasticity and start to feel loose, which is a clear sign that it needs replacing.

SPORTS BRAS

A well-fitting sports bra should feel snug, but not so tight that it affects your breathing. Look for broad, non-elastic straps that won't cut into your shoulders. Padded straps will give extra comfort. Make sure that the underband of the bra fits firmly around the rib cage so that it doesn't move when you are walking or reaching up.

Light support Cropped-top bras can be worn as outerwear and have compressed cups fitted inside. These flatten the breasts against the body, keeping breast motion to a minimum, and are most suitable for women with smaller breasts. Cropped-top bras often have reflective strips on them so you can be seen in the dark. The 'Y-back' panel on the back gives good support for all sizes.

Firm support Sports bras with moulded cups that encapsulate each breast give firmer support, and are ideal for women with fuller breasts. Avoid sports bras that hook together at the front, as these tend to allow more breast motion. Look for pull-on types, or ones that hook at the back. The 'Y-back' panel again gives good support, and the open design allows a greater area of skin to breathe freely.

Socks

The subject of sports socks is one that never fails to draw debate among power walkers. Some people swear by thin socks, but I personally find they don't give my feet enough protection and I would always advocate thick socks with extra padding (*see box, below*). Whichever type of sock you choose, stick to synthetic fibres that will wick away moisture and dry quickly; cotton or wool socks can cause blisters when they get wet. Make sure that your socks are a good fit, not too tight and restricting, and reach high enough to cover your Achilles tendon. Replace your socks as soon as you can see that they are wearing thin on the heels or elsewhere. Never wear your shoes without socks. You will soon be complaining of blisters, friction burns, and athlete's foot – not too mention smelly shoes.

LOW-CUT ANKLE SOCKS

These may look elegant, but very low-cut socks are not recommended for power walking. As you stride, your Achilles tendon continually hit the back of the shoes, and without high ankle socks you risk getting blisters.

WHICH SOCK TO CHOOSE?

There are so many styles of sports socks to choose from nowadays that I can only recommend that you try a selection until you find the right one for you. You may need to spend a little extra for good walking socks, but they are worth the investment. Nothing beats wearing a great pair of socks in the right-fitting shoes. Always choose synthetic fibres over natural ones; they are better at drawing moisture away from your skin.

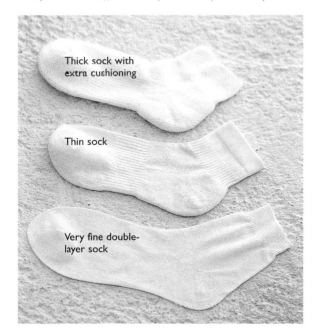

Thick sock with extra cushioning

Thin sock

Very fine double-layer sock

Thick socks with extra padding These are my favourite type of socks. They feel soft and luxurious, and have extra padded areas at strategic points on the foot, in the ball and heel, and sometimes over the arch of the foot, too. Make sure you wear them when buying shoes as thick socks can make up to half a size difference.

Thin socks Look for minimal or no seams, and check that they are made from a synthetic fibre. Thin socks made from cotton quickly get wet and lose their softness. Some people find that thin socks cause friction and don't give enough protection to the foot. However, many people do like them, so go with what works for you.

Double-layer socks These are made with two layers of fabric and are designed to prevent blisters. The theory is that as you move, the two layers rub against each other rather than against your foot. I feel that they are more successful for runners than for walkers.

BASIC EQUIPMENT

One of the benefits of power walking is that you do not need any specialist equipment. As long as you have on a good pair of shoes, you can open your front door and set off. However, for your own comfort and safety, and certainly if you want to keep an accurate track of your progress or take part in walking events, there are a few pieces of basic equipment that you will find helpful.

Pedometers

Whether you are an absolute beginner or an experienced power walker, pedometers can be very useful. The basic function of these small devices records each step that you take, then multiplies your total number of steps by the length of your stride to get the distance you have walked (for more details on pedometers and measuring your stride, see pp36–37). They are worn clipped onto the waistband of leggings or shorts, or on a belt above the hip.

Unless you have a pedometer that is designed to record movement over hilly terrain, they are more reliable used on the flat where you will have a consistent stride pattern. Pedometers are an excellent tool for motivating beginners because they provide hard proof of progress, and they are ideal for more experienced power walkers for training

purposes. Digital models are available, but I find the mechanical models just as good. When you are starting out all you need is a basic pedometer, but there are models available that, for example, will also calculate how many calories you have burned, announce at intervals how far you have walked, or act as a heart-rate monitor. For fun, try wearing a pedometer for 24 hours to see what distance you cover in a day. The alternative to a pedometer is to wear your watch and use this to time your walking pace and calculate distance (see p37).

Walk bags and other accessories

For safety reasons, you should always wear a bum bag when you go out power walking, no matter how short a distance you plan to go. Use it to carry essentials such as keys, money, lip salve, sunglasses, and even your mobile phone (see also pp116–117). For comfort, make sure that the bag fits into the small of your back and does not flop around as you walk. Bags that also come with a holder for a water bottle are ideal.

If you do not like to feel anything around your waist use a wrist pouch. This is a small zipped purse just big enough to take keys and money and has Velcro straps to fit snugly around the wrist.

Avoid backpacks – they are not good for your posture, and even the lightweight ones will tend to cut into your shoulders. However, if you are trail walking (see pp112–113), you may want to invest in a light backpack with well-padded straps.

WATER BOTTLES

Keeping hydrated is vital when you are exercising, so always take a bottle of water with you when out walking, even if you are planning a short session. (See pp84–85 for more on water.)

For easy handling, a "D-shaped" water bottle that fits over your fist is excellent, or buy a bottle with a sports drinking top from which you can easily take sips of water.

Some reusable water bottles come with their own holder that clips onto your belt. Alternatively, use a bum bag that includes a water-bottle holder.

OUTDOOR EXTRAS

In addition to your bum bag and bottle of water, there are two other important items you need when power walking: sunglasses with UV protection, and a waterproof sunscreen. Apply waterproof sunscreen even on winter's days to protect your skin (see *also* pp114–115). Take your sunscreen with you in your bum bag if you are going for a long walk so that you can reapply it as necessary.

Sunglasses
Protect the eyes from strain and sun damage

Sunscreen
Wear a SPF 15 or above, preferably in a waterproof form

Water bottle
A sports drinking top makes taking sips of water easy

Pedometer
Not essential, but useful to monitor your progress

Bum bag
Wear with the bag positioned in the small of the back

Find a bum bag that will hold all your essentials, including a bottle of water, leaving your hands totally free.

Attach your pedometer to your bum bag, but make sure that it fits snugly onto your hip; if it is loose, you will not get a correct reading.

START WALKING

Before you begin any new exercise plan it is

important to determine your fitness and flexibility so

that you begin working out at a level that is right for

you. By following the easy step-by-step sequences you

will quickly develop the correct walking technique.

Team these skills with the ability to plan the best

routes, and you will be ready to get walking.

"A journey of a thousand miles must begin
with a single step." LAO TZU

HOW FIT ARE YOU?

Whether you are just starting out or are already quite active, it is important to determine your level of flexibility and strength before you begin a new form of exercise to avoid overworking your muscles, or training harder than is healthy for you. Assessing your fitness for power walking isn't necessarily that obvious. If you do an aerobics class three times a week, you may have good stamina but weak walking muscles, whereas if you walk to the bus stop every day, you may have strong legs.

Flexibility and strength

Flexible muscles and tendons are achieved through a regular stretching programme and by including stretches when you warm up and cool down (*see pp52–53 and 68–72*). A full range of motion is important for everyday life, and more specifically to achieve and enjoy a good walking technique.

The calf muscles, the Achilles tendon, and the muscles down the shin are all used in power walking. To test how flexible you are in these areas, sit on the floor with your legs out in front of you. Flex your feet so that the toes move towards you. If they move beyond the point of being perpendicular to the floor, then your flexibility is excellent. Exactly perpendicular is good, and anything less than perpendicular means that you need to work on improving flexibility in your leg muscles.

Establishing how strong you are will help you to determine what stage you need to start your training at (*see pp52–53*). Core muscle strength is vital for your posture, and good posture and stability are essential components of the power-walking technique. The test on the page opposite will help you to assess your core stability strength.

Check your fitness

The heart is the most important muscle in the body, beating more than 100,000 times a day. This unique engine moves blood from your lungs, where the blood collects oxygen, to the muscles, where the oxygen is burnt as fuel. Like any other muscle, the heart needs to be worked to keep it strong and healthy. Cardiovascular exercise, such as power walking, does this by increasing the body's demand for oxygen and making the heart beat faster. Your age and level of fitness are the biggest variables to affect your heart rate. Not drinking enough water while walking, the food you have eaten, tiredness or anxiety can all cause fluctuations and influence the rate at which your heart beats.

Heart rate and exertion

When you start exercising, it is important to know your level of aerobic fitness so that you work within safe and controlled levels of exertion. Your resting heart rate is a good guide to your current level of fitness. The stronger your heart is the more blood it can pump through the body with each beat, which means it needs to beat less at rest, and while exercising, compared to the heart of an unfit person.

LOWER BACK FLEXIBILITY TEST

Lower back and hamstring muscles are important in power walking. To test them, sit on the floor with your legs straight in front of you, ankles flexed, and feet flat against a wall. Reach your hands towards the wall. If your palms reach flat against the wall, your flexibility is excellent. Knuckles to the wall is good, fingertips is average, not reaching at all means stretching is vital.

CORE MUSCLES TEST

This exercise assesses strength in the core muscles. If your back is in neutral, flat to your hand, and does not arch as the leg lowers, this is a good indication that you have strong muscles. The weaker your muscles, the more your back will arch (*see pp54–59*). Return to these exercises every so often to assess your progress. Stop the test if it feels uncomfortable at any point to ensure you don't strain your back.

1 Lie on your back with a neutral spine and place your hands under the small of your back. Inhale deeply and slowly lift your right leg, keeping the leg straight and the foot flexed. When you breathe out, use your core muscles to slowly lower your right leg. As your leg reaches 45 degrees, feel with your hand to check if your back is arching. Repeat on the left leg.

2 If your back didn't arch in Step 1, try this more advanced move. Start in the same position and lift both legs. As you exhale, slowly lower them and notice what happens to the small of your back. Only very strong core muscles will allow you to lower your legs without any movement in your back.

To establish your resting heart rate, sit down for at least 10 minutes, then feel your pulse on your wrist (the radial artery). Hold your upturned wrist with your thumb underneath for support, and one or two fingers placed lightly on the inside of your wrist. Count the beats of your pulse for 10 seconds, then multiply this number by 6 to calculate the average beats for 1 minute.

A fit adult has a resting heart rate of 50–60 beats per minute (bpm). The heart of an average adult beats at about 72 bpm at rest, and an unfit person has a resting heart rate of 80–90 bpm. Some people, though, naturally have a higher or lower heart rate.

Heart-rate monitors

The most efficient method for measuring the heart rate is to use a heart-rate monitor (*see opposite*). They are simple to use and very efficient. Most take into account information such as your gender, age, height, and body weight to give you a realistic idea of your training zone (*see box, below*).

HEART RATE TRAINING ZONE

To work your heart and lungs in the most efficient way, it is important to exercise between 65 per cent and 85 per cent of your maximum heart rate (MHR). If you are a man, 220 − your age = MHR; and if you are a woman, 226 − your age = MHR. For example, if you are a 40-year-old woman, your MHR is 186 beats per minute (bpm).

To find your optimum training zone, work out the upper and lower limit percentages:
65 per cent of 186 (0.65 × 186) is 117 bpm
85 per cent of 186 (0.85 × 186) is 153 bpm
The training zone for a 40-year-old woman, therefore, is between 120 bpm and 158 bpm.

Working out above the upper limit would put unnecessary and unproductive stress on your body. Below the lower limit, you may not be working hard enough and may not see any real benefit from your walking programme.

Once you know your resting heart rate, you can establish what your optimum training zone should be (*see box, below left*). If you are unfit, you should work at the lower end of your maximum heart rate (MHR), and if you are very unfit, you may need to drop as low as 55–50 per cent of your MHR. To continue getting fitter, increase the intensity within the range of your training zone. A strap-on heart-rate monitor is the most efficient way of checking your heart rate while moving.

The Borg scale

This is a system of numbers to describe intensity in exercise (*see below*). The Borg scale relies on your own perception of exertion – how fatigued or not you feel while exercising – and is therefore a quick way of assessing how hard you are working. It is particularly useful for those at a higher level of fitness who are in tune with their bodies. However, beginners may not find it quite as accurate as they may feel they are working at a higher rate than they really are.

When walking at a brisk pace, most people should feel they are working between four and seven on the Borg scale. A person of average fitness would feel that seven is an appropriate level of exertion. If you feel you are working too hard then slow down. If the workout feels too light, try speeding up.

Borg Rate of Perceived Exertion (RPE)

RPE	DESCRIPTION
0	Nothing at all
0.5	Very very weak
1	Very weak
2	Weak
3	Moderate
4	Somewhat strong – endurance training
5–6	Strong – endurance training
7–9	Very strong – strength training
10	Very very strong
*	Maximal

Watch-like receiver displays heart rate

Place one or two fingers lightly on pulse point

The most common type of heart-rate monitor (*top*) consists of a chest strap with a transmitter that measures the electrical activity of your heart and then sends radio signals to a receiver fixed to your wrist. For a manual check of your heart rate, feel the pulse point on your wrist (*above*).

To achieve the best results from your walk you do not need need to push yourself at 100 per cent capacity. Your ideal pace will work your heart between 65 and 85 per cent of your maximum heart rate.

SETTING YOUR STRIDE

To make the most of power walking as a fitness programme, you need to determine your current walking pace. The aim then is to increase your walking speed over time in order to improve your level of fitness. The length of your stride is the important factor here – once you have established the average length of your stride, you can work out how far and how fast you are walking.

Stride length and frequency

The length of your stride is largely determined by the length of your legs, but the degree of flexibility in your hamstring muscles at the backs of your thighs, and the amount of mobility in your hips, will also affect the length of your stride – if these muscles are tight, they will improve the more you walk and stretch your muscles. When you stride in power walking, each step should feel natural and easy (*see also pp42–43*). Beginners often assume that to move faster they need to take larger steps, but the opposite is true. To move faster, keep to a comfortable stride, but quicken your movement

and take more steps per minute. If you feel that you are bouncing as you walk, the chances are that your stride is too wide and you need to shorten it slightly. Experiment with different stride lengths to find the right pacing for you. You should be able to roll from one foot to the other without feeling that you are breaking the fluid movement.

Measuring your stride

To measure your stride you will need a tape measure, a friend to do the measuring, and a space large enough to walk about 20 paces. Walk with your natural stride for a period long enough to get

WHAT DOES A PEDOMETER TELL YOU?

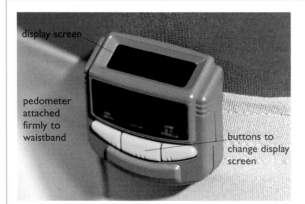

display screen

pedometer attached firmly to waistband

buttons to change display screen

Many pedometers now come with a range of features, including the following, which I find particularly useful for training purposes or for a weight-loss programme:

Calories Pedometers with this feature will estimate the calories burned based on your weight. A great incentive for those wanting to lose weight.

Time Many pedometers have a stopwatch that starts when you take the first step (and can be reset). Others also give the time of day.

Speed Some pedometers will also calculate your average speed, based on how many steps you take per minute.

Alarm This is a useful feature if you are incorporating interval training in your walks (*see p136*). The alarm can be set to sound as a reminder for you to change your pace.

Distance The main function of a pedometer is to calculate how far you have walked in kilometres or miles. Once your stride length has been programmed in, it will count each step you take and calculate the distance walked.

a good rhythm. Stop mid-walk at the point when your feet are furthest apart, at the longest point of your stride. Ask your friend to measure along the ground from your front heel to the back toe: this is the length of your stride. You may want to repeat this exercise a few times to calculate an average stride length. If you are a beginner, your stride is likely to alter over the coming weeks, so it is a good idea to measure your stride again after a few weeks of regular walking. Your technique will improve, naturally quickening your pace and lengthening your stride slightly, and the muscles in your legs and hips will stretch and strengthen.

Steps per minute

To estimate the distance you travel without using a pedometer (*see opposite*) you will need to have

Stop at any random point mid-walk, and measure the distance from the toe of your back foot to the heel of your front foot to establish the length of your stride.

measured your stride. Count the number of steps one foot takes in 1 minute, and then double this figure to get your total number of steps per minute. Now multiply this by your stride length measurement to determine how far you have travelled in 1 minute. The chart below will give you an idea of your current walking pace.

Walking pace	Women	Men
	Minutes per 1.6km (1 mile)	
Easy	17–19 plus	16–18 plus
Moderate	13–16	12–15
Fast	12	11

PLANNING YOUR ROUTE

Great pleasure can be found in spontaneously choosing to go for a walk, but it can also be frustrating. It can be difficult to judge the distance of some walks, which means sometimes a walk can be over too soon, or that you can travel further than you had intended. The key to an enjoyable and successful walk is to firstly, establish your walking ability, and secondly, map out a range of routes that match your level of fitness. This list will grow over time as your ability improves.

Whatever your fitness level in other activities, if you are new to power walking you need to discover your walking ability before you plan any routes. The best way to do this is to walk 1.6km (1 mile), and record how long it took you and how you felt on finishing. If you are concerned that this sounds a long way, bear in mind that on average people walk approximately 4.8km (3 miles) when they do their weekly shopping.

Measure your ability

The ideal place to test your speed and ability over a controlled distance is on a running or athletics track. These can usually be found in schools or parks, and you may need to ask permission to use one. As a general rule, the inside lane of a standard track has a distance of 402 metres (440 yards), but they do vary, so always check the length. To walk 1.6km (1 mile) you will need to walk round the inside track four times. As you move outwards from the inside lane, each track increases in length by about 7 metres (7.5 yards). A track is useful when measuring your ability because there is no traffic to disturb your concentration, there are facilities, such as toilets and water, close by, and it is a safe place to stop if you feel uncomfortable at any time. If there isn't a track near you, the other option is to measure the distance of 1.6km (1 mile) by car or by bike on a road, for you to walk afterwards. Try to make it a circular route so that

you are never far from home, just in case you become tired, or need to stop.

Walk at your fastest pace, but without straining yourself, and time how long this set distance takes you (remember to warm up and cool down, see pp68–72). It may take 15 minutes, it may take 30 minutes or more, or perhaps you will need to stop before the end. When you have finished, assess your progress. For example, could you have carried on walking? Did your legs ache? Was it a struggle, and were you out of breath? The answers to these questions will help you to decide your next move. If you are able to walk 1.6km (1 mile) easily, you are ready to begin one of the programmes (*see pp142–153*). When you start your programme, listen to your body, and if the regime feels too easy or too hard, try another one at a different level. Revisit this test after a few weeks to monitor your progress.

If you struggled to complete the course, you will probably want to walk at your own pace and distance for a few weeks to become accustomed to the exercise. For example, try just one lap of the track, or points on your route for either 0.4km or 0.8km (¼ or ½ mile), see if you can reach either of these markers, and build up from there.

Moving on

Now that you have established your walking ability, and the distance of your start walk, you need to research two or three routes. Some walks will be more successful than others, and it will take a while to build up a list of your favourite routes. Be realistic – if a route takes too much organization, or if you are unsure of the area, then you simply won't walk it. It is important that you enjoy the surroundings. Accessibility, variety, and enjoyment should be your guides when planning walks.

Urban walking

One of the benefits of city walking is that there are usually plenty of level pavements, which allow for a constant stride pattern. There may also be large parks, schools with playing fields, and sometimes even canals to add variety to your walking routes. Do some research about your town to see if you can create a route that will pass some historic features. Check out local maps to see if there is a lake you could walk round, some woodland, or a picturesque view that you could take in. Use power walking to explore your local surroundings and offer you new experiences.

"Mall walking", which is hugely popular in the US, is another option. The benefits of walking in shopping centres is that they provide a safe, climate-controlled environment, complete with facilities. The network of main thoroughfares and side aisles will give you plenty of scope to vary your routes, and to make them as long or as short as you want. Try to avoid busy times of the day so that you don't intimidate shoppers and can allow yourself plenty of room to walk – early in the morning or weekdays are always good times to walk.

The negative side of city walking is concerns about safety. For more information on how to walk safely, see pp116–117.

The great outdoors

If you live in a rural area, your routes may include anything from farmland and wooded areas to forests, hills, and coastline. There is nothing quite like walking in the countryside, with the calming sights and sounds of the natural world all around you. You may find, too, that spotting birds and other wildlife along the way can pleasantly distract you from the effort that you are putting into your workout.

Walks in the country will give you a slightly different, possibly harder, workout if the route involves your walking on dirt tracks or up hills as opposed to flat, even surfaces. Bridlepaths are fine to use in your route, but you may need to watch your footing with extra care because of uneven ground trodden by hooves. Both hills and heavy-going paths will make your muscles work harder over the same distance; bear this in mind if your walk feels tougher than you expected.

There may be less traffic and pollution out of town, but beware because motorists do tend to drive faster on country roads, and the roads can be narrow and without any pavement or verge.

STEPPING IN THE RIGHT DIRECTION

Vary the length of your routes. Even advanced walkers will want shorter routes for when they have less time.

Include surroundings that will suit different moods, from the tranquillity of a park to the bustle of a busy street.

Decide whether you want your walk to start from your front door, or whether you are willing to take public transport out to a new area and walk from there.

If walking at night, check that the area is safe, with good pavements and street lighting. Even during the day, avoid known trouble spots.

Some routes may have heavy traffic and pollution at certain times of the day. Avoid these times if possible.

Establish if there are toilets and shops to buy water if needed on the route, and their exact location.

If your walk goes through a public park, check the opening times.

POSTURE AND BREATHING

The use of modern technology in the work place has led many of us to become more sedentary than ever before, our bodies hunched over desks, reinforcing the very muscles that create poor posture. The best antidote to this is an activity such as walking where good posture and breathing are an essential part of the exercise.

Functional posture

Our core muscles in the back and abdomen (*see pp52–53*) are responsible for holding our bodies upright. However, without constant and proper use, these muscles become lazy and stop working efficiently. Then, when we do try to stand tall and have good posture, it can feel awkward and uncomfortable because the muscles are being asked to do something they are not used to. Standing tall, try drawing your navel into your spine using your

natural corset and notice how your spine automatically realigns. If you do this regularly, you will not only begin to improve your posture, but you will also strengthen and flatten your abdominal muscles, stand taller, and have a more defined shape.

The head-neck-back relationship is key to good posture. The body follows the head, so if your head juts forwards, your spine will follow suit, straining the muscles in the neck,

POSTURE CHECK

Notice how your muscles feel as you bring your body into neutral position.

Incorrect posture The head is thrust forwards, chin jutting out, straining the muscles in the neck and shoulders. The shoulders are slouched and the chest is collapsed. The abdominals are pushed out, arching the spine and throwing the pelvis back.

Correct posture Make sure your weight is evenly distributed, the toes spread to form a stable base. Imagine a straight line from the heel through the back of the knee (not locked). The hips are tilted forwards and the bottom is tucked under. The chest is raised, the shoulders down and relaxed, the neck softly extended. The chin is parallel to the floor and the crown points to the ceiling. The spine is in neutral, which means it is allowed to retain its natural curves.

eyes looking down

Collapsed chest affects oxygen flow

abdominals are pushed out

look straight ahead

chest is raised and open

hip tilted forward

back of knee directly above heel

feet slightly apart

shoulders, and upper back. People who sit a lot, especially in front of a computer, have a tendency to protrude the head and neck forwards.

Often when people start power walking they complain of lower back pain and blame it on the exercise when in fact it is caused by poor posture. It is important to correct posture as early as possible because as we age, bad posture can contribute to all sorts of health problems, from chronic headaches to arthritis.

Breathing

The act of breathing is so natural and automatic that most of us don't give it a second thought. Yet few of us breathe correctly. In general, people use shallow, or chest, breathing and do not use the full capacity of their lungs. Poor posture, too, can restrict the ribcage and prevent the lungs from expanding properly.

> **TIP** A good friend gave me this simple tip to correct posture. Attach an elastic band around something you look at often during the day, such as your telephone at work. Each time you see it, spend 30 seconds squeezing your shoulder blades together. Persevere with this and it will become second nature, strengthening your upper back muscles and in turn help improving your posture.

Breathing deeply using the diaphragm when you are walking will help you to get the most out of your sessions (*see pp76–77 for more on diaphragmatic breathing*). But first you need to get in touch with your breath and experience the energy it brings. Try the breathing exercise below, and as you breathe, mentally send oxygen into the body. Feel the sensation of directing air in and out while the spine lengthens. Practise this until you are able to re-create this feeling when you are out walking.

BREATH AWARENESS

Lie on your back. Lengthen your neck by bringing the chin slightly towards your chest. Your eyes are open and looking straight ahead. Feel your belly button pulling towards the spine. Place one hand on your abdominals just below your navel and the other on your ribcage. Breathe in slowly and rhythmically and be aware of the corset muscles working. Do not allow the abdomen to pop out. Breathe out and feel the sensation of your ribcage moving. Widen the shoulders and feel the shoulder blades moving slightly towards each other. Experience the whole of your upper body broadening rather than moving upwards.

shoulders are relaxed and back

POWER LEGS AND FEET

A few minor adjustments to the way you walk will allow you to easily make the transition from regular walker to power walker. The action of power walking requires that the pelvis and hip area move freely so that the legs can stride out, followed by a pronounced rolling heel-to-toe motion as you move forwards. Work on achieving a good heel strike and a dynamic push off.

1 Stand tall, shoulders relaxed and back, your midsection pulled in, pelvis tipped forwards. Hold your arms loosely by your sides. Now extend your left leg, taking care not to lock or over-extend the knee. Flex the left foot so that the toes point upwards.

2 Take a normal stride length (*see also pp36–37*) and place your heel squarely on the ground with a really good upwards lift on the ankle; this will give you a full range of movement as you roll the left foot through to the mid-stance position in Step 3. Your right, back foot is firmly planted on the ground.

3 Move forwards onto the left foot so that your weight is evenly balanced between the heel of the left foot and the ball of the right foot. Look straight ahead, chin parallel to the ground, and remember to keep your shoulders relaxed.

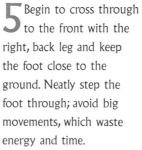

WALKING A LINE

As you take each step, imagine that you are walking down an imaginary line. Your feet should be placed almost directly in front of each other, rather than a wide stance. This saves time and energy as you walk.

4 Transfer your weight onto the left foot, keep the leg straight and keep the weight on your left heel for as long as possible before rolling the length of the foot. Begin to rise onto the ball of the right foot ready for the push off – the most important part of the power walk. The power and thrust comes from pushing off from the toes. It's a challenging move, so begin by exaggerating the push, and feel your leg fully extended from your toes. You may lean forwards slightly at this point.

5 Begin to cross through to the front with the right, back leg and keep the foot close to the ground. Neatly step the foot through; avoid big movements, which waste energy and time.

6 Extend the right leg immediately while raising the foot slightly in preparation to strike with the heel, as in Step 1. As you practise, allow your arms to swing naturally in opposition to your feet (*see also Power Arms pp44–45*).

POWER ARMS

This strong arm movement contributes to a compact and streamlined body, allowing you to move rhythmically and efficiently. Often, people feel self-conscious when they start using power arms, but you will find they are your source of energy and are essential to achieve speed. If you are troubled by poor circulation, good technique will help your hands to stay warm by keeping the blood pumping through them.

1 Stand tall, with your arms relaxed by your sides in the beginner's position. As you start to walk, your arms will naturally swing in opposition to your feet. Experiment with the intensity of your swing as you begin to power walk. Throughout, make sure that the swinging motion starts at your shoulder.

2 This is the neutral position. Your elbows are bent at a 90-degree angle and sit lightly on your waist. Your hands should be relaxed and gently cupped. From the beginner's position in Step 1, progress to walking with your arms in this position. Your elbows shouldn't move as you walk; the movement is from the shoulders.

ensure arm
doesn't cross
the body

hand no lower
than waist-height

tuck elbows
into sides

Both hands should be
lightly cupped.

3 When you are ready, start using
full power arms. To practise, swing
your left arm forwards until your hand
reaches no higher than shoulder height.
Simultaneously bring your right arm
back, your hand just brushing your
waist. Both arms should be square
to the body and elbows bent at
90 degrees. Move with purpose. In this
optimum position, the front, leading
arm should feel as though you are
punching the air, while the back arm
moves with force as though you were
elbowing someone behind you.

WEIGHTS AND WALKING

I advise against people walking
wearing wrist or hand weights
because they can put a strain on
the elbow joints and can create risk
by raising the blood pressure. For
an occasional arm workout, try
carrying two half-filled small bottles
of water. Keep sipping from both of
them so that by the end of your
walk the bottles are empty.

PUTTING IT ALL TOGETHER

Combining power legs and feet with power arms may feel a little awkward at first as you try to keep track of what your feet are doing while making sure, for example, that you don't bring your arms up too high. The only way round this is to start walking and keep practising.

1 Begin with a strong, upright posture, feel your torso lifting from your hips and midsection, eyes looking straight ahead. Check that your shoulders are relaxed and your chest is open. Stand with arms in the neutral position, with elbows bent at a 90-degree angle, and hands lightly cupped.

2 Stride forwards with the left leg, the left ankle well flexed, and ensure that the right, back foot is firmly planted. Start to move the right arm forwards and the left arm backwards, in opposition to the feet. As the left heel strikes the ground, begin to transfer your weight from the right foot onto the left foot.

3 At the mid-stance position, your weight is evenly distributed between the ball of the right foot and the heel of the left foot. Continue to move the arms towards their optimum positions. Make sure that you are looking ahead.

4 Transfer the weight fully onto your left foot as the right foot lifts onto the ball, the toes ready to give you a good push off that will generate your speed. Feel a strong extension in your right leg, your body leaning forwards slightly. At the same time, work your arms to propel you forwards, the right arm punching forwards and the left arm "elbowing" backwards. Watch that your front hand doesn't go higher than shoulder height, and that the back hand doesn't dip below waist height.

5 Lift your right foot and keep it close to the ground as you begin to transfer it to the front. Start to move your right arm backwards and your left arm forwards, again in opposition to the leading foot.

6 Extend the right foot forwards, the toes raised, heel ready to strike; remember to keep your feet pointing forwards as if walking an imaginary line. Swing the arms through the neutral position and into the next cycle.

COMMON MISTAKES

Some of the problems that walkers develop may arise from poor posture. If you suspect that this is true for you, reread the information on posture on pp40–41. If you feel that you are slipping into any of the faults shown below, try checking how you walk in front of a mirror at home and make some adjustments, or ask a friend to watch you while out walking and give you pointers to improve your technique.

Wide and open

This is a common fault, where the arms hang loosely out to the sides, and the feet are wide. Men in particular have a tendency to walk like this. If the lateral muscles are overdeveloped, it is awkward to hold the arms close to the sides. People walking with a wide gait tend to point their toes out to the sides, and consequently the feet roll out to the side. Actively think about how you are using your feet.

Juggling arms

Here, the arms are bent at the correct angle, but as they move the arm going backwards swings out to the side, while the leading arm crosses the body. Keep your arms square and at an equal width apart at all times. The arms should not cross the centre line of your body. Keep your elbows tucked into your waist.

Leading arm too high

As the leading arm goes too high, it also becomes too wide and open, and you may find your feet follow suit. Work on condensing the action of both arms and restricting the thrust of the leading arm.

Leaning forwards

This fault can stem from poor posture, but I suspect that many people lean forwards in the hope that they will travel faster. Bending forwards forces your eyes to look to the ground, which is bad for your posture and can cause injury. Look straight ahead of you and your posture will naturally realign itself. Leaning forwards is often accompanied by another fault: taking too large steps. The assumption here is that overstriding will move you faster, but it has the opposite effect (*see pp36–37*) – the smaller the steps, the faster you will move. To remedy this, keep your arm movements small and your feet will follow.

QUICK GUIDE TO GOOD TECHNIQUE

• Maintain good posture, using your midsection.

• Ensure a strong upward lift on the ankle of the leading foot as it moves to the heel strike.

• Take normal-length strides – don't overstride.

• The heel of the leading foot is planted squarely in front of the back foot.

• Push off well – this is your power point.

• Work your arms from the shoulders, and keep the elbows at right angles at all times.

• Keep your movements compact and streamlined.

STRETCH AND STRENGTHEN

Combining power walking with regular stretching and strengthening exercises will enhance your walking ability and make you more body-aware. As you discover how your body works you will come to appreciate the importance of maintaining core stability. The following moves will start you on the road to stamina, poise, and balance, and a strong and agile body. As soon as you are ready, expand your repertoire of exercises, drawing on Pilates, yoga, Swiss-ball routines, and strength training.

"Truly a flexible back makes for a long life."
CHINESE PROVERB

WHY STRETCH AND STRENGTHEN?

Our muscular system works as a whole to enable us to perform controlled movements efficiently and without stress. For example, when you power walk, you are using all the muscles that run from the gastrocnemius muscle in the calf to the sternocleidomastoid muscle in the neck. Yet from the half-hearted way that many people stretch before and after exercise, it seems few of us appreciate the interdependent relationship between muscle groups, and it's not often that you see someone doing neck stretches before going for a walk.

The muscles responsible for movement are known as skeletal, or voluntary, muscles and they can act in two ways: they can contract and shorten or they can relax and lengthen. Most skeletal muscles work in pairs. The muscles are attached to bones, so when one muscle group contracts, another muscle group lengthens, pulling the bones together or apart and creating movement. Muscles groups are either mobilizing – creating motion – or stabilizing – holding and supporting while other limbs are moving. This is why it is so important to stretch opposite muscle groups, such as calves and shins, and hamstrings and quadriceps.

Flexibility and stretching

Being flexible means that you have good mobility in your muscles and joints. Many factors will have an impact on your flexibility, including your level of activity and whether you work in a sedentary job.

Muscles and joints also become less flexible with age. The way to improve your flexibility, and relieve tension, is through stretching exercises. Before and especially after an activity, stretching (*see pp68–72*) is vital to elongate muscles that have contracted through use. Regular stretching, even for just 10 minutes a day, is a good habit to get into, whether or not you have been exercising.

To get the most out of your power walking, you need flexibility in the muscles you use most: your hamstrings, calf muscles, Achilles tendon, and the muscles in your shoulders and upper back, which you use in the strong power walking arm movement.

Core strength

The core muscles in the back and abdomen (*see page opposite*) help us to stand up and function correctly. In particular, the abdominal muscles, which wrap around the torso and connect the rib cage to the pelvic girdle, keep the core of the body stable and maintain posture. When these muscles are contracted, they act like a corset, keeping the back and front of our bodies in alignment. If these muscles are not used regularly, as in a sedentary lifestyle, they become weak, which leads to poor posture and even shoulder and back problems. By investing in keeping good flexibility and strength, we are not only helping ourselves to stay fit but ensuring a long and active life.

HOW OFTEN?

You should always stretch when you go for a walk (see Warm-up and Cool-down Sequence, p72). If you can, also stretch on days when you are not walking (see also Walking Programmes, pp140–153). For strength, ideally do all the exercises on pp54–59 two or three times a week. There is also a programme of stretching and strengthening you can follow on p73.

WALKING AND POSTURE MUSCLES

The muscles in bold are all the postural muscles that cross all the weight-bearing joints. All these muscles enable you to stand erect and power walk.

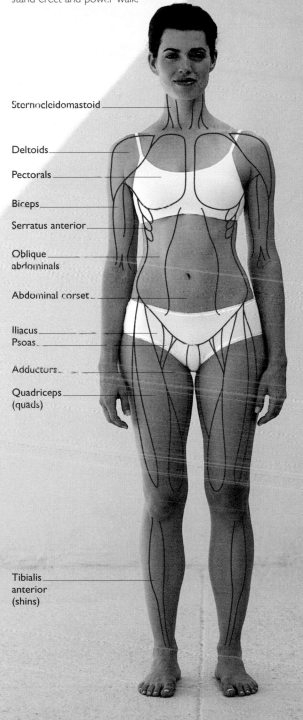

Sternocleidomastoid

Deltoids

Pectorals

Biceps

Serratus anterior

Oblique abdominals

Abdominal corset

Iliacus
Psoas

Adductors

Quadriceps (quads)

Tibialis anterior (shins)

Trapezius

Deltoids

Tricep

Latissimus dorsi

External obliques

Erector spinae

Gluteus maximus (glutes)

Hamstrings

Gastrocnemius and Soleus (calf muscles)

Achilles tendon

DOUBLE LEG STRETCH

This sequence is taken from Pilates. The Double Leg Stretch is a beginner's exercise and is ideal for strengthening the lower abdominal muscles and for challenging your coordination. If you have any problems with your lower back, in Step 2 straighten your legs up to the ceiling instead of holding them at 45 degrees.

1 Lie flat on the mat, your spine in neutral, with your knees bent and arms out to the side, palms facing downwards. Draw both knees up and into your chest, bringing one hand to each leg, with toes pointed. Now, use your abdominals to lift your head and shoulders off the floor. Do not allow your arms to help you lift your upper body. Arms are soft, with elbows out to the sides. Keep your neck long and support it by bringing your chin towards your chest, but maintain some space between them.

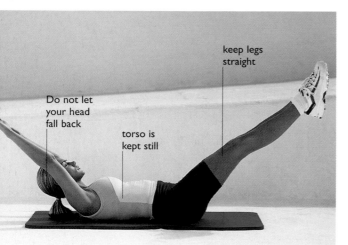

keep legs straight

Do not let your head fall back

torso is kept still

2 Inhale, and reach your arms back behind your ears and stretch your legs out at a 45-degree angle from the floor. Squeeze your buttocks and inner thighs together to support your back. As you stretch your body, imagine that you are being pulled in two directions, with only your abdominals holding you firmly in position on the mat.

3 Exhale and draw your knees towards your chest. Move your arms in a wide circular movement out to each side. Sink your belly further into the floor as though you were trying to squeeze all the air from your lungs. Repeat the sequence 5–10 times. End the exercise by returning to Step 1 and exhaling deeply.

SINGLE STRAIGHT LEG STRETCH

This exercise is also taken from Pilates and can be done on its own or following the Double Leg Stretch. It is a more advanced move that strengthens your core muscles and elongates and strengthens the muscles at the backs of the legs. Start slowly, but with practice the action should be quick, smooth, and rhythmic.

1 Lie flat on the mat with your knees bent and arms out to the side, palms facing downwards. Draw both knees up and into your chest, bringing one hand to each leg, with toes pointed. Now, use your abdominals to lift your head and shoulders off the floor. Keep your neck long and support it by bringing your chin towards your chest, but maintain some space between them.

toes are pointed

2 Inhale, hold your left ankle with both hands, and extend your leg to the ceiling. Stretch out your right leg and hold it at about 45 degrees from the floor. If you cannot reach your ankle, move your hands up your leg (but do not hold behind the knee), and raise the lower leg to a comfortable height. Contract your abdominals and press them into the floor to support the weight of the lower leg – do not use your shoulders for support. Exhale as you switch legs in a scissor-action and hold the ankle of the right leg. Repeat the sequence 5–10 times and end by bringing both legs back to Step 1.

keep head and shoulders lifted

knees are straight but not locked

ROLLING THE BALL

Working with a Swiss ball is a great way to improve your core strength and stability. If you have not used a Swiss ball before, take the following exercises slowly and make sure you feel confident in each position before moving on to the next step. Work on a soft surface and be prepared to roll around. If you have a back problem, seek expert advice before attempting this exercise.

hands are relaxed

knees and feet together

1 Kneel facing the ball, hands flat on the ball, arms bent at the elbow. Roll the ball forwards a short distance until your forearms are resting on top of the ball (you may have to build up to this). Contract your abdominals to support your torso as you balance between your knees and the ball. There should be a straight line from your shoulders to your hips. Hold for 5 seconds, then roll back. Do 2 sets of 5–10 rolls, resting 1 minute between sets.

2 Once you are proficient in Step 1, move on to this more advanced position. With forearms still resting on top of the ball and a neutral back, rise up onto your toes and aim to have your body straight like a plank. Hold for 5 seconds, return to Step 1 and rest briefly. Complete 2 sets of 5–10 sequences, with a 1-minute rest between sets.

keep neck long

pull in abdominals

THE BRIDGE

This exercise also improves your core strength and stability. It works your core muscles and also your glutes and hamstring muscles. Even if at first you don't reach the position in step 2, you will still receive a good work out by attempting it. To receive an advanced workout, lift each leg as described in Step 2. If you have a back problem, seek expert advice before attempting this exercise.

1 Lie on your back, with your arms relaxed by your sides, palms facing downwards. Widen your shoulder blades (*see breathing exercise, p41*). Rest your legs together on the Swiss ball so that your heels and calves are comfortably positioned.

2 Using your core muscles, raise your hips and pelvis so that your body forms a straight line from your shoulders to the tips of your toes. Pull in your buttock muscles and feel your abdominals pressing towards your spine. Keep breathing and hold the position for 15–30 seconds, then return to the start position. Complete 2 sets of 5–10 raises, with a rest of 1 minute between sets. When you are ready, from the raised position, lift one leg off the ball, hold for 5 seconds, then raise the other leg. Watch that your pelvis stays square and does not sink towards the floor.

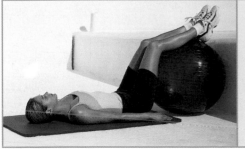

MODIFIED BALL POSITION

If you feel you need more stability to begin with, place the ball against a wall so that it is kept stationary as you do the exercise.

BALL CRUNCH

The secret of balancing on the ball is to calm the mind, focus on the precise
stabilizing point, and make small correcting adjustments. This exercise opens your
chest, stretches your spine and really works your abdominals. If you have a neck or
back problem, please seek expert advice before attempting this exercise.

open your chest

use thighs for support

1 Sit on the ball and walk your feet
forwards until you are lying back
on the ball with your knees bent at
90 degrees. Feet are flat on the
floor, hip-width apart. Let your head
lie back over the ball. Open your
arms wide and let them fall towards
the floor. Draw in your core
muscles to support the pelvis.

2 Place your hands behind your ears, inhale and use your
abdominals to lift your shoulders. Keep the movement
controlled; raise for 4 seconds, hold the position for 4
seconds, then exhale and slowly peel down for 4 seconds.
Repeat 20 times with a rest of 1 minute after the first 10.

keep neck long

SUPERMAN

This exercise is challenging because it requires great control, strength, and balance. Start slowly and have a play with each position. Remember that you will still be working your core muscles while you are wobbling and practising the positions. If you have a back problem, please seek expert advice before attempting this exercise.

balancing point

chest is open

1 Lie face down over the ball with your back in neutral. Hands are flat on the floor with arms shoulder-width apart. Feet should be hip-width apart, but at first have them at a width that feels right for you. Find your exact balancing point on the ball — when you find it you will feel steady and secure.

2 Hold your balancing point. Use the power in your core muscles to raise your shoulders and upper body away from the ball. Stretch your arms out to the sides to help you to balance. Feel your chest opening and expanding. Steady your breath and use it to assist your balance in every step of this sequence.

keep back flat

focus eyes straight ahead

3 Raise your left arm straight in front of you, in line with your body. Straighten your right leg out behind you. Use your core strength to hold yourself still. Look straight ahead, hold for 5 seconds, then switch arms and legs. Repeat on each side 5–10 times.

4 This position is the ultimate in using the pivotal point of balance and takes practice to get right. Raise both your arms and legs. Give the "thumbs up" sign, to activate your shoulder blades for balance. Hold the position for as long as you can, then rest.

UPPER BODY STRETCHES

The upper body, shoulders, arms, chest, and particularly your neck can hold a great deal of tension which can cause stiffness. Stretching restores good mobility and releases a great deal of stress. These upper body stretches are subtle but effective. They should feel pleasurable, so if they are painful in any way, you are pushing too hard. Be aware of having good posture before beginning each stretch.

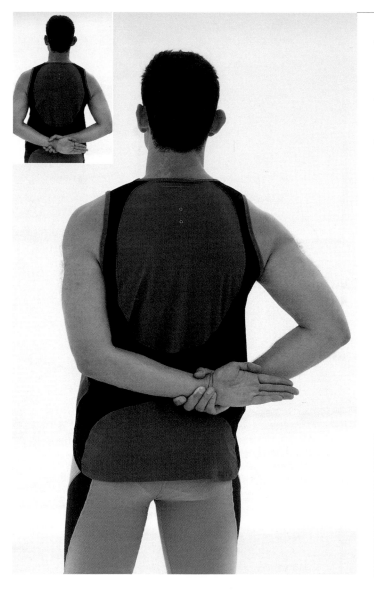

Neck Stretch

Stand tall with your feet slightly apart and knees soft. Move your arms behind your back, with your right hand lightly clasping your left wrist. Keep shoulders straight and gently ease the left arm towards your right arm. You should feel the stretch at the front of the left shoulder. Hold for 10 seconds and repeat for the other arm.

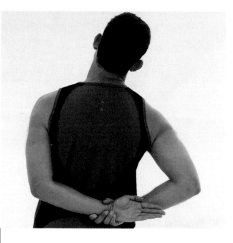

Neck Stretch: Position 2

Tilt your head to the right as you ease the left arm towards the right. You should feel a stretch all the way down the left side of your torso. Hold for 10 seconds, then repeat the entire sequence on the other side.

Tricep Stretch

Stand tall with knees soft
and legs hip-width apart.
Raise your left arm above
your head and bend it so
that your hand is pointing
down your spine. Place
your right hand on your
left elbow and gently ease
your left elbow backwards
to get a good stretch in
the back of your arm. Hold
the stretch for 10 seconds
and then repeat for the
other arm.

Shoulder Stretch

Stand tall with knees soft, and reach up with both arms. Feel a stretch lifting from the pelvis all the way up to your fingertips. Keep your right arm raised and bend it so that your hand is pointing down your spine, palm facing in. Drop your left arm, bend the elbow and interlink the fingers of both hands. Check that your back is in neutral and not arched. Feel the stretch through both shoulders while you hold for approximately 20 seconds, then repeat with opposite arms.

BEGINNER'S ALTERNATIVE

If you are unable to reach far enough to interlink your fingers, hold a belt or small towel to bridge the gap; gradually work at bringing your hands together.

Upper Back Stretch

This stretch releases tension in the upper back, shoulders and neck. Kneel on the floor with knees approximately hip-width apart. Lean forwards to place your hands in front of your knees, palms facing downwards. Walk your hands forwards away from you until your arms are outstretched. Feel the stretch through your spine from your pelvis and deep in your shoulders. Hold for 15 seconds and then return to a sitting position.

ALTERNATIVE

Poor flexibility and tightness in your shoulders and upper back can prevent you from enjoying the full stretch. If this is the case, fold your arms on top of each other and rest your head on your arms. Open your shoulder blades and feel a gentle stretch in your upper back.

LOWER BODY STRETCHES

The muscles and joints in the legs, pelvis, and lower back are going to work hard while power walking, so they need particular attention. It is important to build strength in vulnerable areas, such as knees and ankles, to reduce the risk of injury. You will receive greater benefit from your stretches if you focus on the muscles you are stretching. Little but often is the best policy with these stretches.

Hip Flexor Stretch 1
Stand tall with your feet hip-width apart, then take a step back with your left leg. Place your hands on your right leg for support just above the knee. Lunge slowly forwards onto your right leg, keeping the knee at 90 degrees and above the heel. Keep the hips square and ease them forwards by tightening your buttocks, feeling the stretch in the front of the hip. Hold for 10 seconds and repeat on the other side.

Hip Flexor Stretch 2
Take a normal-length stride forwards with your right foot. Keeping the knees bent, rise onto the balls of both feet, as though you were wearing high heels. Keep your hips square and ease them forwards by tightening the buttocks, feeling the stretch on the front of the hip. Hold for 10 seconds and then repeat on the other side.

Achilles Tendon Stretch
Stand tall with your feet hip-width apart, then take a step back with your left leg. Lean forwards on the right leg into a deep lunge as though you were going in to the original Hip Flexor Stretch. Then rise up onto the ball of your left foot to create a good stretch for the Achilles tendon. Hold this for 10 seconds and repeat on the other leg. This stretch works well when completed following on from Hip Flexor Stretch 1.

Hamstring and Calf Stretch

Stand tall, with your feet together. Step your left leg forwards a normal stride length. Stand with your right foot flat on the floor, toes pointing ahead and left foot flexed. Bend your right knee and place both your hands at the top of your right thigh to support your weight. Lean forwards slightly onto your right foot and sit back into the position. Feel the stretch in your hamstring and calf. To intensify the stretch, sit further back. Hold for 10 seconds and then repeat on the other side.

ALTERNATIVE
Begin the stretch as above, but keep the left foot flat on the floor. This is a gentler stretch for the hamstring and creates a stretch down the shin.

Ankle Stretch

This stretch is taken from yoga, and it is ideal for power walkers because it strengthens the ankles, knees, and hips and increases flexibility in these areas. Sit up straight, with the soles of your feet together. Grasp both ankles and and bring your heels as close to your body as you can. Allow your knees to fall towards the floor – this will get easier with practice. Stay like this for 10 seconds, or longer if you find it comfortable to do so and enjoy the position.

Ensure your feet are touching from toes to the heels.

FULL BODY STRETCHES

The Side Rolls rotate the spine and stretch your obliques (the waist muscles). To advance the Side Rolls, grip a tennis ball between the knees. This will keep your pelvis straight and stretch your obliques more intensely. The Back Stretch gives the spine a powerful stretch and opens the chest.

Side Rolls

Lie flat on the mat with your knees bent at a 90-degree angle, knees close together. Stretch your arms out to the sides, palms facing downwards. Inhale deeply, and as you exhale, slowly turn your head to the right. At the same time, slowly and in a controlled movement, roll both legs to the left. Hold the stretch for about 15 seconds, return to the start position and then repeat on the other side.

keep neck long

shoulders are flat on the floor

abdominals pulled in

Back Stretch

Lie on your front and place your hands directly under your shoulders, with elbows bent and arms close to your sides. Push up from your hands, but keep your elbows bent at around 90 degrees. Hold for 10 seconds, feeling the stretch right down your back. Avoid this exercise if you have any sensitivity or problems in your back.

keep shoulders relaxed

ADVANCED STRETCH

From the lying position, push up with your hands as before. Continue to raise your chest and shoulders, lifting from your hips and midsection, until your arms are straight but your elbows are not locked. Your shoulders should be relaxed, shoulder blades dropped down. Hold for 10 seconds, then return to the start position.

BEFORE AND AFTER WALKING

Warming up and cooling down are essential to prevent aching and injuries to muscles during and after exercise. A short routine will aid flexibility and increase the blood flow into working muscles. Once the muscles are soft and warm, stretching will lengthen them and can help train them to become more pliable. Far from being unrewarding or unnecessary, these exercises are a vital part of your walking programme.

Warming up

Warming up prepares the body for exercise. As you gently exert yourself, your temperature rises and your blood begins to move more rapidly towards the muscles that are being used, which increases their flexibility. Tight muscles are under-used muscles and prone to injury.

If you are quite fit, begin your warm up by walking at an easy pace for 5 minutes. If you are planning a long, demanding walk or if you are unfit you will need a minimum of 10 minutes. Keeping your eyes focused on the path ahead, start to loosen your shoulders and the upper body as you walk, rolling your shoulders a few times. Swing your arms in circular movements and an exaggerated pendulum motion. Your lower body will become warm through the movement of walking. Focus on your body and become sensitive to how it is feeling at that moment. After 5–10 minutes find a suitable spot to stop and follow the Warm-up sequence

(*see p72*). Hold each position for no longer than 10–15 seconds. Breathe deeply and relax into each position as you do it. There should be no pain or pressure, just the sensation of your muscles lengthening. When you have finished, continue walking, increasing your pace gradually over the next 5–10 minutes. If you feel tight during the course of the walk, slow down and stretch again.

Cooling down

The longer and more intense your work out, the longer your cool down will need to be. It is not a good idea to abruptly stop walking as this can cause dizziness.

Five to ten minutes before the end of your walk, begin cooling down. Slow your pace, and once again roll your shoulders and swing your arms. When you stop, follow the Cool-down sequence (*see p72*). This time you can make the stretches deeper and more intense, holding the positions for 15–30 seconds. Take deep breaths and, as you exhale, send the energy to the muscle you are stretching and let the breath take away tension. Do not bounce as this can cause strains. Take care not to overstretch because this can cause a weakness in your joints. It should feel comfortable, not painful. If you know that you have weak areas, work specifically on those places. End your session by relaxing in the corpse pose on p71 (not always possible but a treat when you can).

MIND AND BODY

Warming up not only prepares your body for movement, it also puts your mind in the right frame of mind for exercising. After a hard day's work, for example, the last thing you feel like doing is pounding the streets. A few minutes of gentle walking and stretching has a miraculous way of changing your mind. Conversely, cooling down allows you time to calm and centre yourself before launching back into life.

THE TREE

This yoga position is a personal favourite. It is good for developing your balance, and like so many yoga postures, it also calms and refreshes the mind.

Although it is an unusual choice, I find it is excellent for cooling down and becoming centred. To help you balance at first, place one hand on a wall for support.

drop your shoulders

keep chest open

hips square

1 This exercise should be done in bare feet. Stand tall in a good posture with your feet just slightly apart, your toes spread and your weight evenly balanced between both feet. Transfer your weight onto your left foot and clasp your right ankle. Place the heel of your right foot as high as possible on the inside of your left thigh with your toes pointing down.

2 Focus on an object in front of you, and stretch your arms out to the sides at shoulder height to help your balance. Keep the right knee pointing out to the side and your hips straight. If you feel comfortable, raise your arms in a wide, open gesture towards the ceiling. Keep strong and rooted, yet flexible and relaxed. Hold this position for about 10 seconds and then repeat on the other side.

BACK STRETCH

A supple and flexible back is important for your health and fundamental to any movements that you make. Our backs can become tight, not only by lack of use but also by stress, so spend just a few minutes each day repeating these exercises which will benefit your power walk, and day-to-day health.

keep knees straight, but not locked

2 As you exhale, slowly fold forwards from the pelvis and reach out with your hands. Place your hands on the wall so that your spine is parallel to the floor. Feel the stretch through your back.

1 Stand tall with your feet together, a stride's length from a wall. Inhale and raise your arms above your head, reach tall and lengthen your spine.

arms are soft

3 Exhale deeply and allow your body to drop towards the floor. Feel the stretch down your back and the backs of your legs. Hold for a few seconds, then slowly curl up along the length of your spine to return to a standing position.

Calf Stretch

Stand tall and position yourself facing a wall or doorway. Press the ball of your left foot against the wall with your ankle at a steep angle. Keep hips square, facing front and directly above the heel. Inhale deeply and as you exhale ease into the stretch in your calf. Hold for a few seconds, then repeat on the other leg. Alternate legs, stretching for a total of 5 times on each leg.

Corpse Pose

This yoga pose can remove stress from the spine, leaving the body calm and centred. Lie on your back with your legs slightly apart, arms away from your body with palms facing upwards, eyes closed. Allow your body to feel soft and relaxed. Imagine your breath reaching areas of tension. Remain in the pose for up to 10 minutes, then stretch your arms, roll onto your side, and slowly come up into a sitting position.

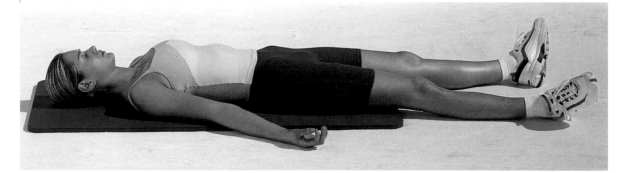

WARM UP AND COOL DOWN

These sequences are essential to prepare the muscles and then return them to a
resting state. Warm and lengthened muscles work more efficiently. Cooling down leaves
your body lengthened and reduces the soreness you sometimes feel after exercise.

Warm-up Sequence

Walk at an easy pace for around 5 minutes
and then do each of these stretches in the
order shown. Hold each position for 10–15
seconds. Distance walkers and those
beginning a fitness programme will need to
walk for 10 minutes before stretching.

Neck Stretch *p60*

Tricep Stretch *p61*

Back Stretch *p70*

Hip Flexor Stretch *p64*

Achilles Tendon Stretch *p64*

Calf Stretch *p71*

Quad and Ankle Stretch *p127*

Cool-down Sequence

Begin your cool down by slowing your pace
5–10 minutes before the end of your walk,
then do each of these stretches in the order
shown for a full cool down. To ensure a
deeper stretch you need to hold each
position for 15–30 seconds.

Hip Flexor Stretch *p64*

Hamstring and Calf Stretch *p64*

Quad and Ankle
Stretch *p127*

The Tree *p70*

Upper Back Stretch *p63*

Shoulder Stand *p77*
(*optional*)

Corpse Pose *p71*

STRETCH AND STRENGTHEN PLAN

Stretching daily will keep you flexible and strengthening is an essential part of a regime. The whole programme should take around 30 minutes. For a shorter programme use either line one or two and finish with line three, or even create your own plan.

Shoulder Stretch p62

Back Stretch p70

Lunges p137

Calf Stretch p71

Quad and Ankle Stretch p127

The Bridge p57

Ball crunch p58

Rolling the Ball p56

Ball squats p131

The Tree p69

Ankle Stretch p65

Side Rolls p66

Single Straight Leg Stretch p54

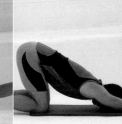
Upper Back Stretch p63

Corpse Pose p71

INNER STRENGTH, OUTER POWER

The more you become aware of your body, the more you may come to appreciate that what you eat and drink, and even the way you breathe, can affect your daily health, energy, and vitality. Examine your attitudes and beliefs and take postive steps to reach your goals.

"Where does the body end and the mind begin?
Where does the mind end and the spirit begin?"

B K S IYENGAR

THE POWER OF BREATH

Breath is life. We can live for weeks without food, days without water, but we can survive only minutes without oxygen. Yet most people are not getting enough of this vital force. They habitually take very shallow breaths through the mouth, and use only the top of the lungs, depriving the body of oxygen. By breathing more fully and deeply we can gain more energy, vitality, and enthusiasm for life. It will not only enhance how we walk, but also contribute to our emotional well-being too.

The mind-body link

The act of breathing has a strong mind-body connection. We know that our state of mind can affect our breathing patterns. When we are frightened or angry, our breath speeds up and becomes irregular. In a totally relaxed state, our breathing becomes slow and rhythmic. In the same way, how we breathe habitually can affect our mood. Shallow breathing through the chest closely resembles the breathing of someone in a state of anxiety, and disrupts the right balance of oxygen and carbon dioxide needed for a relaxed state. Ancient yogis remind us that when the breath is deep and calm, the mind is still, and to achieve this most of us have to work on improving our breathing.

The demands of exercise

It can be quite a struggle, for example, when we are exercising and we find ourselves puffing and panting away. The key is to practise proper breathing before working out, and once on the move, to focus on inhaling and exhaling rhythmically so as not to hyperventilate, which deprives the body of oxygen. The body needs more oxygen when you exercise, and you will find that you naturally increase the number of breaths you take per minute, but you should still maintain a rhythmic cycle of breathing. There is no more exhilarating feeling than when your shoulders are back and relaxed, your chest is open, and your breathing is deep and easy – you will feel that you could walk effortlessly for a hundred miles!

Abdominal breathing

To oxygenate the body fully, we must breathe deeply using the diaphragm (children breathe like this naturally). This is often referred to as diaphragmatic or abdominal breathing.

The diaphragm is a muscle situated between the chest and abdomen. When you breathe in, it moves down to make room in the chest for the lungs to fill with oxygen. As you breathe out, the diaphragm moves up, reducing the chest size, and squeezing air out of the lungs. You are breathing correctly when your abdomen swells forwards as you breathe in, and gently falls as you breathe out, and there is little or no movement in the chest area. Remember, breathing out is just as important as breathing in. The more stale air that you can get rid of as you breathe out, the more clean air you can take in.

CALMING THE BREATH

If you are anxious or your breathing becomes erratic for some reason, try this exercise. Sit upright on a chair, your legs uncrossed, feet flat on the ground. Take a slow breath in through your nose for 3 counts and a long breath out through your mouth for 6 counts. Repeat this breathing cycle until you feel more calm.

SHOULDER STAND

This yoga posture is one of the most important for keeping the body in perfect harmony. It also encourages deep abdominal breathing by limiting movement at the top of the lungs. Do not do this pose if you have high blood pressure, breathing difficulties, or back problems.

1 Lie flat on the mat, your knees bent, arms by your sides. For a few moments breathe in through your nose and out through your mouth, making a soft "ah" sound on each exhale. Inhale and roll your hips off the mat whilst supporting your back with your hands, your knees at right angles to your body. Exhale.

ALTERNATIVE

As you roll up, use a wall for balance. First take one leg away from the wall and when you feel stable, the other.

2 Inhale and take your legs straight up into a vertical position. Try to lift as much of yourself as possible onto your shoulders. Breathe slowly and deeply as you hold the position. Be aware of each breath and how it feels to you. Bring your chin as close as possible to your chest and keep your back straight.

3 To come down, bend your knees towards your head. Straighten your arms in preparation to roll your body back onto the mat. Slowly peel your body down, vertebrae by vertebrae, into the start position. Stay there for a few moments, aware of how you feel and what is happening to your breath.

THINK POSITIVE

Although the focus here is on using positive thinking to achieve your fitness goals, you can apply the principles to any area of your life, including your work, your relationships, your self-image, and your health. The power of the mind to affect physical health has been much talked about, but is there any proof? Well, psychologists in the USA have recently discovered that people who feel positive about ageing live on average $7^1/_2$ years longer than those who see only its downside.

Clearly, the power of thought can have a big influence on our lives, for the better or the worse. We all hold a constant inner dialogue, or self-talk, that can switch from positive to negative and back again. We often choose the negative path, telling ourselves that we are going to fail or that things won't go right. This prevents us from looking forwards to events with happy anticipation, and we may even end up bringing about the very thing we fear.

That negative inner voice can not only prevent us from having the optimism to try to achieve our full potential, but it can also affect our health. Research in Canada carried out over 30 years shows that patients who expect to do well after an operation recover more quickly than those with a pessimistic attitude.

Taking control
So how can we change our attitudes to use the beneficial power of the mind? The first step is to become aware of the nature of our own self-talk.

Psychologists believe that an average person experiences between 20,000 and 60,000 thoughts a day. None of these thoughts is neutral: they are either positive or negative, and they will reinforce themselves day after day.

If you are one of the people who always sees a glass as half empty rather than half full, you need to make a change to positive self-talk to describe your life as you would like it to be. A good way to begin reprogramming your self-talk is to repeat positive affirmations (*see pp80-81*). Make them realistic, so that you can say them with sincerity, and make them in the present tense. Instead of saying, "In six months' time I shall be fit enough to tackle a marathon", say, "Each day I am fitter and stronger."

You will greatly increase your chances of success if you not only believe 100 per cent that you will achieve your goal, but you have a goal that is realistic and achievable, one that is challenging for you, but not impossible.

However, it is important to remember that positive thinking will not magic away all bad things, and it won't do your training for you! Nevertheless, it will help you stick with the programme and deliver the results you want.

DROPPING NEGATIVE LABELS

Reframe your thoughts by changing how you view yourself and how you describe yourself to other people. For example, saying "I'm stupid" will in time make this part of your identity. Instead, think in terms of behaviour, which can be changed. You may sometimes do stupid things, but no one is infallibly wise. Forgive yourself for your mistake and think of the successes that can be balanced against it.

A positive outlook affects your body language, making your posture, your walk and your gestures strong and powerful rather than tentative.

MEDITATE ON YOUR FEET

Meditation is sometimes referred to as an act of mindfulness – that is, the mind is focused on a single point or activity in the present moment. Most people assume that to meditate you must sit cross-legged on the floor with your eyes closed, but it is just as possible, if not easier, to meditate while walking. In fact, walking with awareness in the present moment is a wonderful way to spend time walking alone and can bring great emotional and physical benefits.

The benefits of any type of meditation are well documented and include bringing an inner balance, reducing stress levels, and improving sleep. Meditating and focusing on your breath while power walking is a powerful combination, blending those advantages with fresh air and the acquisition of physical fitness.

Awareness of your movement

Pick a route that is familiar to you, preferably flat, with a tarmac surface, and with little or no traffic, so that walking is easy and distraction is kept to a minimum. Begin your meditation walk by doing a few slow stretches. As you begin to walk, just be aware of the day, the sky, your surroundings, the weather, your energy. Tell your mind that for the next 30 minutes or so you give yourself permission to be totally in the moment.

Pay close attention to your feet and be aware not only of the contact with the ground as your heel strikes it and your balance shifts to the ball of your foot before lifting off again, but also the the contact between your toes and the feel of your sock fabric.

Next, shift your awareness to your ankles, calves, knees and thighs. Notice the way your hips lift and fall as you move, and the swaying of your spine. Feel your belly as the centre of your being and note the intake and output of breath from your chest. Relax your shoulders and enjoy the rhythm and power in your arms and legs as they move together.

With a balanced head position (*see pp40–41*), you will feel the muscles in your neck relaxed and long. Relax your jaw and let your eyes be gently focused ahead. If something distracts you, simply notice it and return your attention to your walking.

Repeating a mantra

Another way to keep your mind in the present moment is to repeat a mantra. This is a word, or group of words, used to keep the mind peaceful and settled. Choose a mantra that feels comfortable and relevant to you, and that will allow your feet to fall into a rhythmic step with each word. While I was going through my cancer treatment, I discovered many, but my favourite is "I am fit – I am healthy".

Repeat your mantra for a minimum of 15 minutes, letting the words fill your head and your feet. There will be times when you will lose your concentration and busy thoughts of the day's tasks and activities will intrude, but quietly put them to one side and reconnect with your mantra.

As you reach the end of your walk, end your meditation and reconnect with your surroundings. Once you have mastered meditating while power walking you will find that you have a restored sense of balance and a mind that is perfectly still.

Looking ahead of you as you walk, take pleasure in the rhythm and swing of your arms and legs as they move smoothly in relation to each other.

WATER

The human body can survive for weeks or even months without food, but without water we would die within days. On average, our bodies are made up of between 65 and 70 per cent water, though that rises even higher in very physically active people, such as athletes, who have a higher proportion of muscle tissue and less fat tissue. Water is our very life source and the amount we drink is crucial to our health – yet many of us regularly drink too little.

Statistics show that as many as one person in four does not drink enough water and is dehydrated. We lose around 3 litres (5¼pt) a day through our urine, faeces, skin, and breath, and although we absorb some water through our food, we need to drink 1.5–2 litres (2½–3½pt) a day to replenish that loss. Too many of us drink tea, coffee, or caffeinated fizzy drinks to quench our thirst, but large quantities of these actually have a diuretic effect instead, apart from being bad for our health. One study has shown that six cups of coffee a day causes a 3 per cent loss of water from the body.

Ensuring that your body is well hydrated will help to keep your skin youthful, your eyes clear, and your digestive system working well. It will also aid in the speedy elimination of toxins from your body and deter cellulite.

Are you drinking enough?

In hot weather, or when we exercise, our bodies dispel heat by means of sweating; during intense activity such as a football or tennis match, fluid loss can be more than 4.5 litres (8pt) an hour, together with a loss of essential body salts such as sodium, potassium, calcium bicarbonate, and phosphate. When you are power walking, particularly if you are taking part in a marathon it is important to remember to increase your intake of fluids.

Some experts in sports medicine believe that it is a mistake to use thirst as your guide, and that by the time you actually feel thirsty you are already dehydrated. Other symptoms of dehydration are irritability and a lack of concentration. Two signs that you are drinking enough water are if you urinate regularly and your urine is a very pale straw colour. Make sure you are properly hydrated before you begin walking.

You will need to replace the fluids you have lost by sweating when you have been power walking, particularly when the weather is hot.

Know your water

Drinking water is essential to maintain good health, and it is better to drink water from any source than not at all, but not all waters are of the same quality. The purer the source of water, the more you will benefit from it.

Filtered water

Activated carbon and ceramic filters reduce the level of impurities in your water, including chlorine, heavy metals such as lead, and sediments, and they will remove the smell and taste of chlorine. Their effectiveness is dependent on the size of the holes in the filter; the smaller they are, the better.

Purified water

The most effective means of purifying water is by an under-sink reverse osmosis system, which removes about 99.9 per cent of contaminants in water, including chlorine, fluoride, nitrates, and lead. The most efficient systems combine activated carbon filtration (*see above*) with the semi-permeable reverse osmosis membrane.

Bottled waters

These come in many guises, and it is useful to learn how to read the labels and become selective. Opt for water in hard plastic bottles or, better still, in glass as some types of plastics can leach chemicals into the water.

Mineral water This is thought to be the best choice because it is natural and untreated, and must come from an officially registered source. By law the label must show the mineral content of the water.

Spring water The content of spring water varies from country to country, and in some cases it is a mixture of natural and treated water. Be aware that some bottled waters are very high in sodium and inorganic minerals such as sulphates or potassium, which in this form are not easily assimilated into the body.

TIP When you get tired of plain water, you can always flavour it. I like to start each day with a cup of hot water with a squeeze of lemon or lime added. This is a great wake-up call for the system. A comforting drink on cold days is to pour boiling water over a slice of raw peeled ginger and let it infuse for 5 minutes. For summertime, leave the ginger-infused water to cool, then chill.

Carbonated water Carbon dioxide gas is added to water in order to emulate natural sparkling mineral water. The carbon dioxide inhibits the growth of bacteria, but once consumed, it turns into carbonic acid, which can contribute to acidity problems in the body.

Oxygenated water This is water to which oxygen has been added. The promise is that this will somehow supply the muscles with more oxygen, thereby enhancing performance. However, so far there is little scientific evidence to support this claim.

Bottled tap water In the USA, if the label states "from a municipal source" or "from a community water system", you can be sure it is simply tap water.

Tap water

The domestic water supply in most developed countries is subject to more tests and monitoring than bottled water. However, many people are wary of the chlorine used for disinfecting tap water as it can destroy the healthy bacteria in our guts. Pesticides and herbicides used at the source can also leach through into the water supply.

Synthetic oestrogens in our water supply, derived from the pill, HRT, and plastics, are another concern as they are thought to be affecting both human and animal fertility.

You can find out more about the quality of your tap water from your local water authority.

HEALTHY EATING

Starting power walking may be the start of reviewing your whole approach to food. As your body grows stronger and more vital, you will want to nourish it with food that gives you the energy you need and the idea of consuming calorie-high, nutrient-low junk food will begin to seem less attractive. So will diets that promise speedy weight loss in exchange for cutting down on the fruit, vegetables and carbohydrates that your body needs.

It often seems that being healthy is associated with depriving ourselves of the foods we love, but in fact good nutrition is a matter of becoming aware of what we are eating and making choices. Jane Sen, an acclaimed writer and lecturer on food and also Dietary Advisor to the Bristol Cancer Help Centre in the UK, has a way of making getting to grips with a healthier diet very simple. She asks two key questions: "Did it once have roots in soil?" and "What happened to your food before it reached you?"

Foods with roots

Without doubt the very best and most nutritious of all our foods are those that started life with roots; they are full of phytochemicals and micronutrients that not only supply our bodies with everything they need, but are easier to digest and absorb than any other foods. Jane's advice is that every time you eat, whether it is beans on toast, curry, or Sunday lunch, always make sure that at least two-thirds of the food on your plate started life with roots in soil.

If the goal is to maximize the amount of plant-based foods that you eat, then it is also to reduce the foods that do not have roots, such as meat, dairy products, and saturated fats. The latter are normally of animal origin and tend to stay solid at room temperature. Eating saturated fats is linked to heart attacks, strokes, and various cancers.

You should also avoid partially hydrogenated and hydrogenated vegetable oils found in hard and semi-soft margarines. These highly processed fats contain synthetic saturated fats known as trans fatty acids, which have been linked to heart disease. Many products contain hydrogenated fats, including bread, cakes, biscuits, ready-made meals, and even french fries and doughnuts from fast food outlets.

Nevertheless, our bodies do need some fats to help in the absorption of vitamins and to give us essential fatty acids (EFAs). The polyunsaturated and monounsaturated fats derived from plants actually act as a preventative against heart attacks and possibly cancer too. So too do the omega-3 fatty acids from fish oils and flaxseeds or flaxseed oil.

What happened to your food?

When it comes to buying food, what we get is often a lot more than we can see. For example, wheat is sprayed with fertilizers and other chemicals many times, and then, unwashed, is made into our bread. Our humble lettuce looks harmless but can be contaminated with a cocktail of artificial chemicals, while the ready-prepared foods that are so handy when we come home tired from work are often high in salt, preservatives, and other additives. Wherever possible, buy foods that are organic and prepare them at home. Substitute wholegrain versions for refined products such as white flour, rice, and pasta.

Aim for the best

It is unrealistic to imagine that because you decide to change your diet you will never succumb to another chocolate or fried breakfast. My philosophy is to be selective when you have these treats and make informed choices. If you eat chocolate, eat the best organic chocolate, and if you have a fried breakfast, use the best ingredients, with little or no oil. Treat coffee in the same way. Use freshly ground organic coffee beans, and savour each sip. This may mean forgoing your regular brew from the coffee machine at work, but if this means you drink less coffee, all the better. Make it a rule to yourself to have the best to be your best.

Eating our five portions

Most of us are aware of governmental advice that we should be eating five portions of fruit and vegetables a day. The estimate is that it could help to prevent 20 per cent of life-threatening illnesses such as heart disease and cancers, but many of us are not sure what constitutes five portions. In fact, a portion is approximately 80g (2¾oz). The following are some useful examples of what constitutes one serving:

- 1 medium apple
- 1 medium banana
- 1 orange
- 3 heaped tablespoons of carrots
- 1 cereal bowl of lettuce
- 1 tomato
- 2 florets of broccoli
- ½ large courgette
- ½ pepper
- 4 heaped tablespoons of French beans

Wherever possible, choose foods that are full of the nutrients that you need – for example, fish for omega-3 essential fatty acid, and nuts and vegetables for protein, calcium, and vitamins.

VITAMINS AND MINERALS

We are often told that if we eat a well-balanced diet with five portions of fruit and vegetables a day we will get all the vitamins and minerals that we need – but medical opinion is divided, with some nutritionalists believing that modern-day living requires us to supplement our diet. Certainly, in our busy lives it can sometimes be difficult to fit in those five portions, but we can boost our intake of vitamins and minerals on a daily basis by drinking juices and taking nutritional supplements.

Vitamins and minerals are essential for good health. Although we can manufacture a few vitamins in our bodies, we extract most of the vitamins and all of the minerals we need from our food. Although we require only minuscule

amounts, a single deficiency can be dangerous; most famously, sailors used to succumb to scurvy until it was discovered in the 18th century that providing a supply of citrus fruits would prevent it.

Vitamins cannot be assimilated into the body without minerals. Together these two vital substances, along with carbohydrates, proteins, fats, and water, provide you with all the essential nutrients for cell growth, tissue repair, organ function, energy, and food utilization.

Fruits and vegetables are a rich source of vitamins and minerals, although vegetables do have the edge with more nutrients. Once again Jane Sen has a suggestion as to how you can gain maximum benefit, and that is to "shop by colour". By reaching the checkout desk with a basket full of different-coloured produce you will not only have the fun of consuming a wide variety of foods, you will also be giving yourself a huge amount of nutrients.

Natural supplements

Unfortunately, many of the foods grown today have depleted vitamin and mineral content as a result of intensive farming practices, and there is a further loss during transportation and storage. Organic food fresh from the soil is the ideal – and

Blended drinks made of fruit and vegetable juices are packed with vitamins, minerals, and enzymes to boost your energy. They are a delicious way of increasing your water intake too.

even when our intake of nutrients is sufficient, they can be easily destroyed by factors such as stress, smoking, taking antibiotics, and living in a polluted atmosphere. Opinions vary as to whether taking nutritional supplements is useful or not, but my own view is that they contributed to my recovery from cancer. A high-potency multivitamin and a separate dose of vitamin C would suit most people, but it is advisable to visit a nutritionist for advice or carry out some research into your own requirements first. Buy the best-quality supplements you can afford – the better brands usually have superior ingredients in well-balanced doses compared to cheaper makes – and make sure that the ingredients are from natural sources. Avoid synthetic vitamins, which can cause toxic reactions and can actually contribute to poor health.

The benefits of juicing

Raw fruits and vegetables that have been juiced retain vitamins and enzymes that are often destroyed in the cooking process. Juicing machines and juicing attachments for food processors are now widely available, and the more expensive models will produce the best results with the tougher vegetables. Many are fiddly to clean, so check this aspect before buying or juicing may come to seem like a chore. There are many books available on juicing where you can find combinations for specific purposes.

WHERE TO FIND SOME OF YOUR MOST IMPORTANT VITAMINS AND MINERALS

Vitamin A	Apricots, cabbage, carrots, curly kale, egg yolks, fish-liver oil (from an uncontaminated source), mango, melon, spinach, squash, sweet potato, Swiss chard, yellow peppers, watercress
Vitamin B group	
B1 (thiamine)	Beans, bran, most vegetables, whole grains, yeast
B2 (riboflavin)	Eggs, leafy green vegetables, mushrooms, tomatoes, wheatgerm
B3 (niacin)	Cabbage, cauliflower, mushrooms, tomatoes
B5 (pantothenic acid)	Alfalfa sprouts, avocadoes, broccoli, cabbage, celery, eggs. lentils, mushrooms, squash, tomatoes
B6	Bananas, broccoli, brussels sprouts, cabbage, cauliflower, lentils, nuts, onions, squash
B12	Eggs
Vitamin C	Citrus fruits, broccoli, cabbage, cauliflower, kiwi fruit, melon, papaya, peas, peppers, sprouted seeds, strawberries, tomatoes
Vitamin D	Egg yolk
Vitamin E	Beans, broccoli, raw leafy green vegetables, peas, pine nuts, sunflower and sesame seeds, unrefined corn oils, wheatgerm, wholegrain cereals
Folic acid	Avocados, broccoli, cashew nuts, cauliflower, hazelnuts, spinach, walnuts, wheatgerm
Calcium	Almonds, brewer's yeast, cabbage, dried beans, green vegetables, nuts, sunflower seeds
Iron	Dates, dried beans, egg yolks, miso, nuts, oats, pumpkin and sesame seeds
Selenium	Brazil nuts, broccoli, cabbage, courgettes, haricot beans, lentils, mushrooms, wheatgerm
Zinc	Almonds, Brazil nuts, brewer's yeast, egg yolks, oats, pumpkin seeds, rye, wholewheat

FOODS FOR FITNESS

Your diet won't turn you into an athlete, but it will help your body to perform at its best. Exercise burns up energy in our bodies, and to achieve results it is important to make sure that you have sufficient fuel to sustain that energy. Exercising when you have not been eating the right foods is like putting your foot down on the accelerator and suddenly finding you have no power.

It especially important when you are putting extra demands on your body that you nourish it with the right foods. These are carbohydrates that break down slowly in the body (*see below*), such as whole grains, beans, and lentils; vegetables and fruits, which are particularly rich in phytochemicals, and protein. Top of the list is water (*see pp84–85*). Dehydration can lead to muscle fatigue and loss of coordination, so it is vital when you are exercising to increase your intake to more than the recommended eight glasses of water a day.

Carbohydrates

The best fuel for sustained exercise is carbohydrates, which are broken down to glucose in the body and stored primarily in your muscles and liver as glycogen. This is then converted back into glucose to provide fuel for the muscles you are exercising. The body can only store a certain amount of glycogen and it cannot be transferred from resting muscles to those that are working, so the glycogen in the muscles you use as you power walk will become depleted quite rapidly. Consequently, it is important to keep your levels topped up, and to have a carbohydrate snack immediately after exercise to speed recovery.

Although all carbohydrates are converted to glucose in the body, the rate at which they are absorbed differs widely. Foods such as beans, legumes, and whole grains are absorbed slowly and will provide fuel over the longer term, making them ideal foods if you are going to undertake strenuous exercise.

A green approach

Studies have consistently shown that people who eat a vegetarian diet live longer than meat eaters and have lower incidences of many major diseases, including cancer, heart disease, and diabetes. Yet many people have concerns about meeting all their nutritional needs through a vegetarian diet, especially when they are active in sports. It is sometimes thought, for example, that an athlete needs to tuck into a large steak to gain sufficient protein, but in fact most of us in the West consume far more protein than we need, and just a few almonds provides the equivalent protein in an average steak. We can all obtain the proteins we need from many plant foods, including soya, pulses, grains, and all nuts and seeds. A word of warning: do not replace meat with equivalent amounts of cheese since it is high in saturated fats.

Eating a wide range of plant-based foods will provide you with a high intake of antioxidants and phytochemicals, all of which have innumerable health-giving properties. They will also provide a good source of calcium (found in, for example, raw broccoli, sunflower seeds, almonds, and Brazil nuts), which is vital for strong, healthy bones and keeping active.

Eating for a marathon

If you have been following the food guidelines and training plans set out in this book, your body will be in good shape to take on the challenge of a marathon. Even so, it is important to take care with your diet right before and right after the event.

The week before

By now, training will be minimal, which will decrease the use of glycogen. Keep your food light and simple. Eat plenty of vegetables, steamed or roasted, and include one vegetable juice or smoothie a day. Salads with light dressings, grilled fish (or very lean meat), and plenty of unrefined carbohydrates such as potatoes, rice, or quinoa are ideal. Avoid rich sauces, spicy dishes, fried foods, big meals that are heavy to digest, and alcohol, which is dehydrating. Eat every 2–3 hours, using cereal bars as snacks, and drink plenty of water, so that on the day of the event you are well hydrated and need only sip small amounts on a regular basis.

The day before

Make sure you have two good high-carbohydrate meals. Always try to eat your largest meal in the middle of the day, so that your body does not have to work hard at digestion through the night.

The Big Day

Have a good breakfast of cereals or pancakes and fruit about two hours before the start. Apart from water, it is wise to take something that will give you a burst of energy, such as a banana, raisins, energy bars, or glucose tablets. Do not try any unfamiliar foods or you may only achieve an upset stomach. You should also avoid anything salty or dry, such as nuts.

Immediately after the event, eat a carbohydrate snack such as a sandwich or muffin to aid your recovery and choose a carbohydrate-led meal for the post-event dinner.

ENERGY-BOOSTING FOODS

Brown rice Unrefined brown long-grain rice is a complex carbohydrate with twice the fibre and nutrients of white rice. It is the best rice for slow absorption. As well as being a good source of protein, it also contains zinc, magnesium, vitamin B_6, and selenium.

Bananas They are one of the richest sources of potassium, which helps to regulate muscle contractions. Bananas will replenish the potassium lost through sweating and are therefore an ideal snack when you are exercising strenuously.

Broccoli This is high in fibre, and is a good source of iron and folic acid. Iron helps to bind oxygen in red blood cells, which is then transported and used by the body's muscles, organs, and tissues. Folic acid is important for the health of red blood cells and keeping cholesterol levels under control. If eaten raw, broccoli also provides calcium.

Beans and legumes Dried beans, peas, and lentils make superb low-burning foods that are also high in protein and are a good source of folic acid (see *Broccoli, above*).

Carrot juice When freshly juiced (see p89) it is a concentrated source of vitamin A (beta carotene), which is essential for the growth and repair of body tissues, and will help to fight infections.

Dried fruits These are an excellent concentrated source of energy and are rich in iron (see *Broccoli, above*) and calcium. They are high in fructose and very sweet, but they make a good snack to put in your bum bag.

Papaya This exotic fruit has as much potassium as bananas (see *Bananas, above*), as well as high levels of vitamin C and beta carotene (see *Carrots, above*).

Pasta Choose wholewheat or buckwheat pasta when you are looking for slow-burning fuel for your muscles. A pasta dish is the perfect pre-marathon meal. Pasta also provides iron, and the B vitamins thiamine, niacin, and riboflavin.

Potatoes A medium-sized portion of this powerhouse vegetable provides twice the potassium of a banana (see *Bananas, above*), and is high in vitamin C and iron (see *Broccoli, above*). They are excellent for boosting blood energy levels and fighting fatigue.

WALKING FOR YOU

Whether your main objective is to raise money for charity, care for your body during pregnancy, lose a little weight, or just have fun days out with your family, walking has the answer. It is one of the easiest and simplest ways in which you can bring fitness into every day of your life, regardless of age or ability.

"Walking is a delectable madness,
very good for sanity." COLIN FLETCHER

FIT WALKING INTO YOUR DAY

Most of us live busy lives, our days filled to the brim. How, we ask ourselves, can we possibly squeeze in one more activity? With power walking the answer is, very easily. You can slot in a walk at any time to suit you, and it can be as long or as short as you want it to be. Once you are committed to a regular walking programme, you may be surprised to find that you have more energy and greater mental clarity, and that you are more productive and efficient in the same amount of time.

How many times have you promised yourself that you will visit the gym, or start a fitness regime but failed because you put other things first, leaving no time to carry those good intentions through? Usually, work, children, or other commitments come first, leaving little time left for us to spend on ourselves. Yet if a friend asks for a favour, we usually find the time to help. So, why are we never that kind to ourselves?

Many of us expend much of our energy on others, both physically and emotionally. There is nothing wrong with doing this, as long as we make time for our own needs too, such as hobbies, pampering, and exercise. Walking is one of the easiest, most accessible, and rewarding ways of giving back to ourselves. You can do it anywhere, and you don't need anyone else. The rewards come fast, and there are no rules governing how long you do it for and when, because even a short walk will have an impact. You also don't have to rely on a club or gym. Walking fulfils all the essential criteria for a busy person.

In truth, we can all find the time to do something if it is important enough to us. The secret to fitting walking into your life is to change your perspective on how you spend your time and to accept the value of allocating time for yourself.

Be realistic

With many things in life, it is far better to go for quality rather than quantity. The amount of time you spend dedicated to your health and fitness is no exception to this. Be selective with your time, and be thoughtful about choosing how, and when, you spend the time you have set aside for yourself. The greater enjoyment you receive while walking, the more you will benefit from it. There is little

point in striding out for an hour, only to feel guilty and stressed on your return because there were other things you should have been doing. It is better to be realistic, walk for less time, and be able to leave all your concerns behind.

Apply time-management skills, prioritize the tasks in your day, and learn how to say no, and you will notice a big difference. We often waste precious time being overwhelmed and stressed, rather than calmly deciding on a plan. As a starting point, try to find 30 minutes, preferably at the same time each day, and make it sacrosanct to walking. You will soon be guarding the time jealously, and everyone else will accept it as part of your routine. To find the time, you could walk the children to school instead of driving, walk to an appointment, get off the bus or train to the office a stop earlier than usual and walk the rest of the way, or even rise half-an-hour earlier in the morning. You decide when you take the 30 minutes, but make sure you always do it.

Be prepared

Have a selection of different routes planned and ready (*see pp38–39*), including a short route for days when you have only 15–20 minutes free. Try to plot some of the routes through a park or woodland, so you can spend time within a calming atmosphere and remove yourself from everything. Also plot a route near your work so that you won't need to spend time wondering where to go if you find time to walk during your lunch break. Keep a second set of kit at work so that there really are no excuses for missing a chance to walk.

Book an appointment

One way to create time for walking is to book in walking sessions in your diary. If each walking appointment is blocked out in pen, you can make other commitments work around them, and only

---

FINDING TIME TO WALK

Less is more: a short walk may be more enjoyable and fun than a long walk that takes up too much of your time and leaves you feeling stressed and under pressure.

Be creative with your time, and walk part or all of the way when you would otherwise use transport.

Be prepared by arranging some walking routes. A variety of walks is a big key to motivation.

Make an appointment with yourself for a walking date and stick to it; learn how to say no to others.

Join a walking group, form one of your own, or find a walking pal; shared activities are easier to manage.

---

reluctantly should you have to give up your walking times. You can tell people that you have an appointment at that time, but you don't need to say what it is for. Your 30 minutes of walking might not sound that important to them, and you could find yourself being persuaded to alter your plans. Doing this will also raise your awareness of any other spaces in your week when you could take additional time for yourself.

Get some allies

One of the best ways to fit walking into your schedule is to join a walking group (*see p97*). You could join one that exists locally, or even form a group of your own. Group members will encourage you to turn up, which will motivate you to attend regularly. Alternatively, try to find a like-minded person who has a similar lifestyle to yourself. If you have children, perhaps a shared babysitter will solve the problem of time. If you work shifts, maybe you can meet others who want to walk late at night. Make a walk a social event, work together on a training plan, and book a regular time and place to meet.

ONE, TWO, THREE OR MORE

Power walking is a sport that works whether you want to train on your own, with a friend, or as part of a busy, demanding life, walking alone may give you precious breathing space. On the other hand, time spent power walking with a friend is always filled with fun, motivation, and good conversation. Joining a walking group is a popular way to combine walking with a social life.

Going solo

Walking alone is one of the greatest pleasures of power walking. With no one else to consider, you can test your personal best time, walking at speed to your own rhythm, and feel the power and exhilaration of using your body. I relish an unaccompanied walk when I want to let off steam at the end of a busy day, or if I'm building up speed for a marathon.

If you have a problem to solve, going for a solitary walk provides you with the perfect opportunity to think things through without any distractions. Your body can pound along on automatic pilot, leaving your mind free to ponder. I usually find that after about half an hour of turning over an issue in my mind, I almost always have a solution to my worry.

Many people find that walking alone is conducive to creative thinking. Before you set off, prime your mind to focus on a given subject, but as you start walking switch your attention to your

surroundings. Let your senses open to everything around you: people, buildings, animals, flowers, trees. Keep a steady, easy pace, don't try to force inspirational thoughts, but trust that they will float up from your unconscious to your conscious mind, naturally and effortlessly. Take a small notepad and pen in your walk bag so that you can jot down your thoughts. A variation on this theme is to walk while you meditate (*see pp82–83*).

Make sure when you are walking alone that you pick routes where you feel safe from traffic or people (*see also pp116–117*).

Tête-à-tète

Walking with a friend will often get you out of the door when you lack the drive to do it yourself, and will ensure that you walk regularly and more often. Plan routes and training programmes together so that you are both equally involved. Take it in turns to act as the pace-setter so that you don't reach a fitness plateau. Working at improving your fitness also gives added purpose to your walks.

Talking while you are walking makes the time fly by, and it is a good benchmark for exertion (*see also pp34–37*). If you are able to carry on a conversation with no difficulty, then your pace may be too easy. At a moderate to high-intensity pace, you should be able to keep talking, but you may be slightly breathless. If the talking stops and you are out of breath, then you are pushing yourself too hard and should slow down.

WALKING FOR ONE

Plan your walking routes carefully when walking alone to be sure you do not veer into an unsafe neighbourhood. Take all the usual safety precautions and always let somebody know where you are going. Walking alone can be an inspiring, empowering experience, but it is no fun if you do not feel safe.

Part of the crowd

Apart from the camaraderie that a walking group brings, it also provides a constant source of encouragement and support, and a steady flow of banter and laughter. The feeling of belonging and having a common purpose that comes with being part of a group is irreplaceable. Meetings offer a social occasion, a chance to meet like-minded people, and often the means to form lasting friendships. Invariably, the larger the group, the more mixed the abilities will be. Try to pair up with those of a similar walking ability or a little better than you, which may mean splitting the group into a number of smaller groups. If this happens, arrange meeting points to regroup.

Walking groups are usually informal affairs, arranged between friends or work colleagues. However, more formal walking groups and walking clubs do exist, and you may find notices about meetings for these at your local sports centre or in your local newspaper. Most clubs charge a small fee for membership to cover administration costs.

Walking with a friend is a great way to keep motivated and stick to a training programme. It can also turn exercising into a social occasion.

WALKING TO LOSE WEIGHT

If the average person power walks four times a week, for 45 minutes a time, he or she will lose approximately 8kg (18lb) within a year, without changing his or her diet in any way. Add to this programme regular stretching and strengthening workouts, together with a healthy, weight-aware diet, and you will have the tools you need to reach your ideal weight, and feel fantastic too.

Keep a log

Whether your goal is to lose 2kg (5lb) or 22kg (50lb), there are three promises that you must make to yourself to reach your target. The first is to keep a daily log. For the first week, simply note down everything that you eat without making any changes to your diet (*see Healthy foods, opposite*). For the following three weeks, use your log to chart what you eat as part of your diet, how much and when, how far and how fast you walk, and how you feel. You must be completely honest with yourself, and include every detail no matter how small. By doing this you can build a realistic picture of your weaknesses and strengths, and can act accordingly.

Note in your log your ideal, and realistically achievable, weight for a month's time. Aim to lose 0.5–1kg (1–2lb) a week on average – any more than this, and you are losing water and muscle, not fat. Don't be disheartened if your weight loss is slow at the start of a diet. This is normal, especially when teamed with exercise, as this builds muscle, and muscle tissue weighs more than fat. How well your clothes fit can act as a good guide to weight loss. Weigh yourself once a week only, at the same time, as your weight can fluctuate on a daily basis.

Power walking burns calories efficiently, and will tone and shape your body. Eat a wide variety of healthy foods, but watch quantities when you are trying to lose weight. Keeping a log can help you discover if you are overeating and why, and chart the success of your exercise plan.

Get moving

The second promise you need to make is to start exercising. The principle is simple: exercise aerobically to burn calories and you will lose weight, even without changing your diet. Power walking is a low-impact, aerobic exercise that burns about 300 calories an hour for the average person weighing 70kg (150lb) and walking at a brisk pace. (The faster you walk, or the heavier you are, the more calories you will burn.) Power walking also builds muscles, and the more muscle mass you have, in ratio to fat, the faster your metabolism works. Your metabolic rate is the speed at which your body naturally burns calories (energy), even when sleeping. So not only will you lose body fat

by walking, you will also develop the muscle that will keep it off.

For weight loss, it is recommended that you take 10,000 steps a day, of which 4,000–6,000 steps should be uninterrupted walking. Use a pedometer to record the number of steps you take and count the number of calories burnt (*see pp36–37*). A heart-rate monitor (*see pp32–35*) will ensure that you raise your heart rate sufficiently to burn fat. Use the Weight Loss Programme (*see pp152–153*) as a guide for your walking routine, which includes stretching and strengthening routines.

Healthy foods

The third promise is to start making healthy changes to the way you eat. I don't personally advocate any kind of quick-fix diet as they give short-term results generally and deny your body the complete range of foods it needs to stay strong and vibrant.

It may be that you don't need to go on a food-reduction regime at all. For one week, make no alterations to your diet, but write down daily everything you eat to give you an idea of your normal intake, and make a note of your walks.

At the end of the week, you may find that power walking alone is starting to give you the improved body shape you were hoping for, and you don't need to watch the amount of food you are eating. However, you may still need to make changes to the types of foods that you eat. For example, slowly replace any refined, highly processed foods with healthy alternatives, such as brown rice or pasta instead of white, and include more vegetables, wholegrains, and pulses in your diet.

Even if you need to reduce portion sizes, always eat breakfast to give your metabolism a kick-start. Eat five to six small meals a day to keep your energy levels up and your metabolism steady, and to help avoid hunger pangs. Drink plenty of water (*see pp84–85*). Dehydration can give the illusion of hunger instead of thirst, and can be a cause of weight gain. Plan ahead what you will eat each day, keep an eye on fat and sugar content, and chew your food thoroughly. Don't deny yourself treats, but save them for special occasions. The success of a weight-loss plan depends on your being aware of what you are eating, making the right choices, and taking small steps to success.

WALKING AND PREGNANCY

Keeping fit and healthy throughout pregnancy will give you much-needed energy and help you to feel less tired. Walking is a low-impact, non-contact form of cardiovascular exercise that you can continue doing right into the later stages of pregnancy. It will keep your muscles strong and flexible, which is invaluable during both pregnancy and labour.

If you are already a walker, carry on but walk less intensively, even in the first few months. You should always discuss exercise with your doctor first in case of complications. If you are new to walking and were fairly inactive before you became pregnant, again consult your doctor – if you are very unfit, this is not the time to start an exercise programme. This is especially important in the first trimester when you may feel super-charged with energy. Try to walk three times a week, and build up to 20–30-minute sessions.

Keep in tune with your body and if you feel overtired, short of breath, or uncomfortable, stop immediately. Keep your walking routes close to your home and amenities, in case you tire easily. Drink water before, during, and after your walk.

Alter your technique

Walking during pregnancy requires some adjustments to your technique. During and just after pregnancy your body releases the hormone relaxin, which softens and loosens your joints in preparation for childbirth. This newly found flexibility can lead to overextending in stretches and in other activities if you are not careful. It may sound wonderful to be so agile, but be cautious to avoid injury and don't push your body too far.

During pregnancy, walk with a shorter stride than usual to create a less aggressive movement in your hips. Ensure your workout is low-impact by keeping your feet low to the ground as you walk. Note that marathons are not recommended for women at any stage of pregnancy.

Walking by trimester

In the first trimester (weeks 1–13), you can more or less follow your normal walking routine, but start to reduce the level of intensity. Don't walk in hot and humid weather as studies indicate that overheating may cause birth defects.

In the second trimester (weeks 14–26), to avoid straining your back, watch your posture (*see pp40–41*), and remember to look ahead. Don't walk on uneven ground, such as trails and beaches – stick to tarmac. Check in the second and third trimesters that your shoes are supporting your arches, which will be under pressure as your weight increases. Your feet may also swell to the point that you need shoes in the next size up.

In the third trimester (weeks 27–40), keep going for as long as you can. You will need to slow right down; don't push yourself to walk further than you feel comfortable.

WALKING WITH YOUR BABY

About 4–6 weeks after the birth, you should be able to resume walking. You might like to carry your baby with you in a carrier or use an all-terrain buggy, but be aware of your posture. Keep your arms bent and push with your body weight, not just your shoulders. For an older baby or young child use a well-fitting backpack or carrier as it is better for your posture and technique.

THE RAISED CAT STRETCH

This stretch is based on a yoga pose and is perfect for stretching your lower back and strengthening your legs without putting any strain on the abdomen. It develops balance and focus, and has the effect of making you feel powerful and strong. Use it to replace the full body stretches on pp66–67.

1 Begin by kneeling with hands below shoulders and knees below hips. Keep arms straight, but without locking the elbows, and eyes looking down. Check you are comfortable in this start position.

2 Inhale and slowly lift your right leg up and out behind you, pointing your toe and raising your head at the same time. Feel it work the back of the leg and notice the stretch along your spine.

3 Now bend your right leg and point your toe. Exhale slowly and hold the position for a few seconds. Inhale and lower your leg, returning to the start position in Step 1. Repeat on the other side. Once you are familiar with the sequence, steps 2 and 3 can be completed in one fluid movement.

WALKING WITH CHILDREN

Physical activity is essential to a child's healthy development. The earlier you can introduce regular exercise into your child's life, the greater the chance that he or she will carry this pattern through into adulthood. Walking – whether power walking or simply brisk walking – with children is a great way to get them moving. You will provide them with an important role model, and firmly implant the idea that walking is a natural and normal activity.

Statistics show that children in the developed world are becoming more sedentary, overweight, and unfit. Less sport is played at school, and more time is spent in front of televisions and computers than ever before. Physical activity behaviour patterns are established while young and it is vital that parents, along with schools, encourage children to get moving. Current recommendations are that they should do at least 30 minutes of moderate-intensity physical activity each day, such as playing outdoors, dancing, doing sports, cycling, helping with everyday active tasks, such as gardening, and, of course, walking. These activities allow children to learn motor skills, develop fitness, increase energy expenditure, and also enhance academic performance and mental health. Start walking with children as early as possible, even if it means carrying them in the first year or so (*see pp100–101*).

In addition to walking, introduce as many fun exercise activities as possible that will encourage children to move their bodies and develop their motor skills.

WALKING TO SCHOOL

Physical activity early in the day clears away the cobwebs, and will make you and your child alert and ready to face your day. It may not be possible to walk your child to school, especially if the journey is long, but if you can, it is also a great way of spending special time with your child. If you find it more convenient, you may be able to organize a walking rota with other parents, and take turns to supervise a group of children to school.

At some point your child may ask to be allowed to walk to school alone. Never allow him or her to walk a route you haven't checked out together with your child first, and that you have established is a safe one. Time the journey so you know how long it should take your child to get home. Always make sure that he or she has a walking pal there and back, or better still walks with a group of children.

Walking safely is essential. Check out the organizations on pp154–155 for more information on children and walking to school safely.

Make walking fun

Set aside regular times for walking, from 30 minutes to an hour, at least once a week if your child is already fairly physically active, and up to three or more times a week if your child is turning into a couch potato. Most children aged between three and seven years will make good walking companions. If you power walk, albeit at a slower pace, so will they. As a rough guide to how far you can walk with small children, estimate 1km (½ mile) per birthday. This means a three-year-old should be able to walk 3km (2 miles) in total, but allow for plenty of rests, and accept that some children are more physical and stronger than others.

Children will walk further when there is something to see and do along the way, so try different routes (*see pp38–39*) that take in, for example, parks, streams, and woods. You may want to collect interesting things along the way, or play I-spy. Plan your turnaround point at a playground, or even a toy shop. If children associate walking with fun activities, they will want to go again. Always remember to carry extra water for your children.

For older children, devise routes that require simple map reading. They will love to be in charge of where to go next, and you can teach them a useful life skill at the same time. Gadgets are usually a source of fascination, so walking with a pedometer (*see pp36–37*) is bound to appeal. Have a chart at home so they can record their progress, and you may like to add a reward system of stars.

Walking events

Most children enjoy non-competitive walking events, especially if it means coming away with a medal or a T-shirt. Many charity walking events are ideal for families and are a way to share your hobby with your children. They will especially enjoy raising money for others, so try to ensure that they are sponsored, no matter how small the final sum.

Walking is a great activity for children. Explore beaches, parks, and woods, or even try walking in the rain. Variety in surroundings and games will keep them entertained.

Tuning into teenagers

Walking is an ideal way for teenagers to control their weight healthily and sensibly. Teenagers need challenges, so activities such as hiking (*see pp112–113*) or orienteering are good ways to keep them active. Orienteering is a sport that involves quickly navigating your way between designated control points marked on a map. It is a great way to explore the countryside, and can be quite physical, depending on the terrain. Check to see if there is an orienteering club in your area that organizes a range of events.

Walking events and marathons often have an under-17 category. These tend to be popular and well attended.

WALKING FOR CHARITIES

A rewarding and positive way to set a challenge for yourself while giving you an incentive to get fitter is to take part in a sponsored walk. By entering a charity event you will be joining many like-minded people in actively raising money and awareness for a worthy cause. Of the thousands of charities worldwide, the causes vary from the environment, wildlife, disease, childcare and others. There will almost definitely be an event near you that suits your ability and concern.

For first-timers

As a starting point, if you have a favourite charity, approach it to find out whether it is involved with any walking event coming up. If you have a specific distance you would like to walk, do your research with this in mind. Before agreeing to an event, be sure that you are prepared to commit to the training. Some events are very popular and have limited entry numbers, so for you to drop out at a later stage would mean lost sponsorship money for the charity. Bear in mind that a marathon will require you to do around three months training, while 10km (6 miles) may take only three or four

weeks to train for. Browse the Programme pages for guidance on training schedules (*see pp140–153*). There are a multitude of sponsored walks and "strollathons" that you can take part in, and something to suit every ability. For the short-distance walker, beginners, or those wanting a less demanding challenge, there are plenty of 5km (3-mile) and 10km (6-mile) walks, which are ideal distances. If you are a stronger walker, you may want to get to the front of the walkers or start early and ensure that you don't get blocked in by families and those walking at a slower pace. There are also running events of this distance which are also fine for walkers to take part in.

At this point, you might also want to think about whether you would rather walk alone or with a team. Training becomes more social in a team, and means there is always encouragement at hand.

Sponsorship

With larger events, the demand to enter usually far outweighs the available places. Charities often have their own allocation of places and these are available to anyone provided you are willing to commit to raising a specified minimum amount of sponsorship money for that charity, although in

Walk the Walk organizes the Moonwalk to raise money to support cancer research and good health. The walk starts at midnight and has thousands power walking through the night.

some cases the amount can be quite high. Before you confirm your entry it is important to think about whether or not you will be able to easily raise the sponsorship money required. To maximize your money-raising ability, try posting your sponsor form on the internet. Your chosen charity should be able to advise you on this and give you additional fundraising ideas.

Once you have entered, read carefully through the information that is sent to you, and make a point of checking where you will find water, toilets, and First Aid stops. Check out the time the event will close on the day. Some half-marathons, for example, are only open for three hours, which means this is the longest walk-time allowed, so training will be essential if you want to finish in time. However, other events are not so demanding, and are more geared for mixed ability and families.

Once you have completed the walk, collecting the sponsorship money can be very time-consuming. Ask if sponsors would like to make a small donation instead so that you can collect the money at the same time as they make their pledge to save you visiting each person twice.

Go further afield

If you have completed a shorter distance and enjoyed the experience, expand your horizons and try a 16km (10-mile) event, a half-marathon (21km/13 miles), or a full-marathon (42.2km/ 26¼ miles). There are events taking place throughout the world most weekends, so you will have plenty of choice. You may wish to stay local, but for those who are keen, there is an extra challenge in travelling to another country.

With overseas events, if you aren't tied to a specific cause, search for one that guarantees to refund your travelling expenses (this will be subject to you raising a specified amount). The result is a great exchange because you get to travel and the

The start of a marathon is very exciting. Write your name on your T-shirt or top so that supporters can cheer you on. Crowds can really motivate if you are flagging near the end.

charity receives much-needed funds. For those who want to push the boundaries, there are three-day hiking challenges in America, a back-to-back marathon on challenging terrain in South Africa, a walk that takes in the Great Wall of China, and many 161km (100-mile) races. Some of these events are primarily for runners, so check that as a walker you meet their rules and be sure you are fit enough for the time regulations. Walk the Walk, my charity, is a power-walking charity that organizes teams for a variety of challenges, from 5km (3-mile) walks and marathons, to walking the Inca trail. The Moonwalk, a night-time marathon, is very popular and is spreading worldwide.

COMPETITIVE WALKING

Entering for a competitive event is an excellent way to keep you motivated and focused. Make sure that you set yourself a challenging, but achievable, goal; no matter how many times you have raced, it is always exciting to cross the finish line to receive your medal. If you are a fast power walker and you would like to push yourself that bit further, discover a different type of challenge altogether with either speed walking or racewalking.

Most competitive races take place on roads and are primarily for runners, but these are still ideal for power walkers to take part in. Some marathons now even offer a walker's category. Often a fit and fast power walker will match the pace of a runner, so don't be discouraged from entering. However, it is important never to accidentally block in a runner and prevent him or her from passing.

Road races are fun events, and many double as money-raising avenues for charity (*see pp104–105*), although some people will be taking part simply to win or gain a good recorded time. There are many

Racewalking is the recognized sport for walkers. It is a sociable sport with clubs worldwide that organize races over a range of distances.

NO LAST-MINUTE CHANGES

Many people make the mistake of wearing new clothing or, even worse, new walking shoes on the day of their marathon or competition walk. My advice is to keep everything exactly the same on the day as it has been in training, including your clothes and equipment, so that you won't get any shocks on the day. Shoes in particular need to be worn in to ensure minimal blisters.

different lengths of races that are organized, so you can start with a shorter distance and build up to a marathon over time.

Entering a marathon

Never underestimate the training needed to ensure you finish a marathon. A marathon is 42.2km (26¼ miles) long, and can take on average between five and ten hours to complete, which is a significant amount of time to be on your feet. You should allow yourself a minimum of three months to prepare, particularly if you are aiming for a good finishing time. If you have never walked before, you will need to allow longer to train, anything from 12 to 18 weeks. You will find a full training programme for walking a marathon on pp150–151.

Fifty per cent of walking a successful marathon is in your mind and the belief that you can accomplish it. Depending on your level of fitness and power-walking ability, your aim should be to walk at a fast and constantly maintained pace over the entire distance. You will also need to modify your diet towards the end of your training. For advice on what you need to eat and drink on the days leading up to the marathon, see pp90–91. On the day, wear your usual training clothes (*see also box, top*). Comfortable feet are vital to your performance (*see pp18–23*). Smother your feet with petroleum jelly as this is an excellent way to prevent blisters (*see also p128*).

Speed walking and racewalking

When you reach a consistent walking pace of 8 km/ph (5 miles/ph) or more, you naturally feel that you want to start running. This is because running is the easier way to move comfortably at high speed initially and it is also your body's natural energy-saving option. However, if you do continue walking instead and push the body that little more intensely, you will find that you are speed walking. Speed walking is a milder, slower form of racewalking, just the same as jogging is to running. Interestingly, both speed walking and racewalking use more energy and burn more calories than when running. It is relatively easy to progress from power and speed walking to racewalking, but it will help if you can join a club to receive coaching on the racewalking technique (*see pp150–153*).

There are two main rules in racewalking that must be strictly adhered to. Firstly, a walker must maintain contact with the ground at all times. This means that the leading foot must be planted before lifting the back foot. Secondly, the knee of the leading leg must be kept straight from the moment each foot touches the ground until the leg is vertical. These restrictions result in your hips rotating as your weight shifts from side to side, and consequently gives racewalkers their unique wiggle.

Racewalking is an endurance sport but, like power walking, it has the benefit of being low-impact and therefore has a low risk of injury. It is a very sociable sport with clubs all over the world. Members are always eager to enlist new walkers and very willing to help all levels and ages of newcomers.

Racewalking is a major sport and is represented in the Commonwealth and Olympic games. Clubs will cover distances from 1.6 km (1 mile) to 161km (100 miles) or more

OUT AND ABOUT

You can power walk almost anywhere, at any time, which makes power walking one of the most accessible ways to keep fit. Even extreme weather need not be a deterrent, as long as you have the right clothing and equipment for the conditions. Try combining road walking with hill walking and include other types of terrain for some of your walks. These will not only challenge you physically, the variety in your walks will also keep you motivated.

"An early-morning walk is a blessing for the whole day."
HENRY DAVID THOREAU

ROAD WALKING

Roads and pavements are easily accessible for walkers. The advantage of walking on tarmac or paving is that the surface is generally flat and even, which means less strain is placed on ankles and knees, so the risk of injury is reduced. Road walking is particularly ideal for interval training. While it is possible to interval train on any surface or terrain, the more even the ground, the greater the opportunity to concentrate on your speed and technique.

If you are considering taking part in a long-distance walking event, you will need to have experienced training on tarmac because most events will take place on roads. As part of your training, you a may want to introduce interval training, which will help to increase your fitness levels.

Interval training

Your heart is a muscle that needs to be trained like any other, and this is what interval training is designed specifically to do. The training involves alternately walking for periods of time at a high intensity (faster) and periods of low intensity (slower). This increases your fitness and aerobic strength and stamina. The periods of intense walking should feel like all-out exertion, and the slower periods are designed for you to recover your breath and composure ready to repeat another interval of intensity.

Interval training is extremely effective at burning fat. The harder periods will work your body at a high level that raises your metabolic rate (*see pp98–99*) enough to continue burning fat (calories) for up to 18 hours after your walk.

Begin as you would for any walk by warming up and stretching (*see pp68–72*). Once you are warm

and have a good flow to your walk you can begin interval training. The length and intensity of both the fast and slow intervals will depend on your level of fitness. The extra stress put on your heart through this training means it is not ideal for someone with a low level of fitness, so check with your doctor to determine if it is suitable for you.

The intervals at a faster speed should be short bursts and can last from 30 seconds to 3 minutes. The slower-speed intervals are longer and can last 2–15 minutes. As a guide, start with a ratio of 1:2, so for every 1 minute walked at an intense, fast pace, you should double it for the slow, recovery pace. If it feels too tough or too easy, adjust the length of intervals accordingly. As your fitness improves, try a ratio of 1.1, so that the periods of fast and slow walking are equal in length.

Each of your fast and slow periods should be of a similar intensity throughout the whole walk. Don't start with a pace so fast you won't be able to repeat it at each interval. Complete your session as you would any walk by cooling down and stretching (*see pp68–72*). Interval training is challenging and should be limited to a couple of times a week. You will find it beneficial to keep a log (*see pp158–159*) to monitor your progress in interval training.

A treadmill (*see pp136–137*) is useful for interval training because accurate monitoring of the length and speed of each interval is easy. Treadmills are sprung, so softer to walk on than other terrains.

Walking on roads and pavements prepares you for long-distance events and is the perfect surface to carry out interval training, a fat-burning high-intensity aerobic cardio workout.

TRAIL WALKING

Walking on trails in different terrains can make a pleasant change from road walking. In particular, conquering hills is a great way to increase the intensity of your walk, improve your endurance levels, and burn more calories. You will also test your core stability when covering uneven ground. To get the full enjoyment and benefit of this type of walking you will need to make changes to both your technique and clothing.

The most demanding part of trail walking is usually navigating hills, and you will need to prepare for this. Approach hill training in the same way as road walking, by starting slowly with short walks and building up from there. Begin by including more hills in your road power-walking routes, or increasing the incline on your treadmill a little. Over a period of about two weeks or so, your legs should become accustomed to the change of angle. Unfortunately, there is no easy way to prepare your body for walking downhill, and consequently even strong walkers are sometimes surprised by how difficult they find it.

Changes in your technique

To assist you in walking up a hill, shorten your step to use your body more efficiently and lean forwards slightly as the incline becomes more acute. To descend, again keep your stride short and lean back a little, but not too far. Going down a hill sounds easy, but this is just as challenging as going up because the impact of your body weight increases from 1.5 times your normal weight to 5 times your normal weight. This puts extra stress on your limbs and joints, and to begin with you may even find it a little painful.

Walking on rough ground can work out different parts of your body. On uneven surfaces, you will need to consider a change in your shoes and clothing.

SAND WALKING

Walking barefoot in sand is a great way to massage the soles of your feet. With or without shoes, it also offers the benefit of strengthening your ankles and toning the muscles in your legs. The action is similar to walking up and down hills because the angle of your ankle is exaggerated. As your foot sinks into the sand, more energy than normal is required to lift the foot with each step. It is also easier to develop and beware of a strong heel-to-toe action, which is integral to the power-walking technique. If you find that walking on soft sand is too tiring and hard work for your legs, try walking on the harder, compact sand found nearer to the sea. While you are at the beach you can also take advantage of the resistance that the sea gives as you walk along the shore. Walking in shallow water acts as a resistance 12–14 times stronger than in air. Keep close to the beach as you walk to ensure you don't lose balance in water too deep.

Your ankles, knees, hips, and lower back will all help to stabilize you and will take the strain of walking on uneven ground. Your outer-thigh muscles (abductors) in particular will be working much harder than usual. Focus on strengthening the muscles in these areas and your core stability muscles to give you maximum support (*see* pp54–59).

Clothes and useful extras

Your shoes are key to your overall comfort, particularly if you are going to be walking at awkward angles on uneven terrain for continuous periods of time. When walking off-road, it is better to wear a shoe that is durable and has deep treads for good traction. A Gore-tex shoe is very light, protective, and waterproof. Allow ample room for your toes, because your foot will slide forwards in your shoe as you walk downhill.

For rugged trails and walking in winter, wear a rigid, waterproof hiking boot that covers your ankle to give maximum protection and support so your ankles and knees don't twist. Whatever your footwear, get used to it – its weight, and the way your foot moves inside it – before going out on a long walk.

Where the hikes are less challenging, you can wear the same clothes as for power walking (*see* pp24–25). However, you may want to substitute a lightweight walking trouser or a pair of shorts for your leggings. When you are walking in hills, a warm sunny day can become cold and wet very quickly, so be prepared with a windproof jacket, a fleece and waterproof clothing. With more extreme conditions, it is advisable to get expert advice on specific equipment (*see also* pp114–115).

When out for the day, take a small backpack rather than a bum bag, which may be too small to carry everything you need. Practise walking with a rucksack on your back for a few flat road walks first to get used to the weight. You will need plenty of water, some food, insect repellent, waterproof clothing, a detailed map of the area, the safety items on p116, and a compass. It is important that you are able to read a map and understand the symbols before setting out.

Walking poles can be useful on rough or steep ground. They come in varying weights, and today some are surprisingly light. The poles are most useful to aid your balance, particularly on a descent.

Finally, a note on safety. As trail walking becomes more known about, it is probably wise not to walk alone. Go with a friend or join a group.

WALKING IN DIFFERENT CLIMATES

Extreme weather can be a challenge, but rarely are the conditions so bad that you need be prevented from enjoying your walk. Heading out on crisp new snow or with the sun warming your skin can be a great experience. For a walk to be a success in extreme heat or cold, it is important to be prepared by wearing the correct clothing, knowing your limitations, and learning all you can to make yourself safe and comfortable.

Always check the weather forecast so that you can decide if a walk is possible that day and prepare for the conditions. Even the fittest person will have days when a walk is out of the question. Note that temperatures above 35°C (95°F) or below -23°C (-10°F) are always unsafe.

When walking in extreme heat, be cautious and slow your pace down if the temperature is above 26°C (80°F). Also check the humidity level. High humidity can push the apparent temperature up to 5°C (10°F) because the moisture in the air prevents your sweat from evaporating, and it is the evaporation that cools you. Heat stroke and heat exhaustion can be very serious. To avoid suffering from either, walk at the coolest times of day, before 11.00am and after 3.00pm. You may need to slow your pace and keep alert to how you feel. At the first sign of dizziness or a headache, stop walking and cool down.

In the same way, be aware of the wind chill factor, which can turn a cold day into a freezing one. In cold conditions your heart has to work extra hard for you to walk and keep warm. If you have a heart problem, you should consult a doctor before walking in very cold weather. To avoid the most severe conditions, try to walk in the middle, and warmest, part of the day.

Keeping cool in the heat

When walking in heat always drink plenty of water to stay hydrated. Your body will sweat more than in normal weather, and can need as much as double your normal intake of water to replace lost fluids. Drink 0.6 litres (1 pint) of water both before and after your walk and drink regularly during your walk, at least every 15–20 minutes.

While preoccupied with walking, you may be unaware of the sun's intensity until it is too late. Wear light or white clothes to reflect the sun's heat, and choose those that are made from moisture-wicking fabrics. Invest in sun-protective clothing if you can; their sun protection factor (SPF) ranges from SPF 30 to SPF 100. Wear clothing that covers the body rather than exposing it. A hat is essential, preferably one that covers the back of your neck, and you should always wear UV protection sunglasses. Apply a suitable strength sun cream

---

TIPS ON KEEPING COOL

Freeze half a bottle of water and top it up with cold water before you set out. You will then have a cool drink, at least until the ice melts.

For a cool head, soak an old cotton hat in cold water, and make holes in it to release the heat.

To keep your body cool, use a plant sprayer filled with water to mist your walking top. The dampened material will keep you cooler for longer.

TIPS ON KEEPING WARM

Alter your stride so that your pace is shorter and quicker to raise the heart rate and keep you warm.

Always wear a hat that covers your ears – 60 per cent of your body heat is lost through the top of the head.

Carry a small, hand-held hot pack to warm your hands if you really feel the chill.

If you have asthma you may want to breathe warm air, so wear a scarf to cover your chin and mouth.

liberally all over, even under your clothes, then re-apply later, because sweating will rub it off.

Protecting against the cold

In cold conditions it is essential to warm up and stretch thoroughly before setting out. Do your cool-down stretches indoors, and after your walk change out of your clothes quickly to avoid getting a chill.

Wear two or three layers of thin thermal garments. These will trap warm air between the layers and keep you warm, and can be removed if you get hot. A flexible waterproof jacket with underarm and side zips will give you the option to let your body breathe. An attachable hood with a peak is a must, with drawstrings to fit it close to your head – most ski jackets are ideal. Wear thermal longjohns underneath your leggings, but nothing that restricts movement. To keep your feet dry, invest in sturdy, waterproof shoes with good sole grips in case the ground is treacherous underfoot. You may have to accept less flexibility in your shoe, and consequently less speed, but it means you can continue walking.

In cold weather, wearing mittens combined with a strong arm movement will help your upper body and hands to stay warm as you walk.

SAFETY

Whether you are walking in a busy city or down quiet country lanes, alone or with a walking group, you need to walk with safety in mind. Unfortunately, most of us live in societies where we need to be cautious and careful, especially if living in a big city. No one wants to walk constantly looking over their shoulder, so use your common sense combined with a few simple precautions and you will always be prepared and be safe.

The secret to a safe walk is forward planning. First, you need to make sure you have packed your bum bag with essential items. Secondly, plan your route carefully. Thirdly, you need to make sure you can be seen if you are walking at dusk or at night. Follow these guidelines and you will feel more in control, relaxed, and confident when walking.

Essentials for your walk bag

The following may seem like a lot of items, but they are all small and should be taken on every single walk. Choose a bum bag that is compact, but will carry all you need (*see also pp28–29*). Ideally it should have separate pockets, in which you can store items such as medical information and important contact telephone numbers. You could even write these details with permanent ink on the inside of your bag, since that way you will never lose them. Make sure you have a small amount of money with you, enough for a taxi ride home if needed or for extra water. Have a few coins for an emergency phone call, and don't forget to replace the money when you spend it.

Invest in a small tub of petroleum jelly to rub onto your feet in case your shoes begin to chafe, and for your lips if they become dry or chapped, especially in extreme weather. Plasters or pieces of lint-free dressing are useful for any minor accidents, and tissues always come in handy. Some paper and a short pencil are a useful inclusion for noting down something special you see, or for taking notes on your training or routes.

The only items you will need to replace in your bag every time you walk are something to snack on

Kit yourself out for walking in the dark with fluorescent strips attached to your clothing, footwear and hat. It's essential to be seen and recognized as a moving body.

such as a banana, a bottle of water, your keys, and your mobile phone if you own one.

Check out the area

It's great to walk alone, but if some of your walks travel through areas you are wary of, you may prefer to walk with a friend. Winter in particular is difficult because of limited daylight hours, so a walking group can be a good option. If you are walking alone always let somebody know where you are going and when you expect to be back. When out, walk tall, head up, and with confidence, and you will look much less vulnerable. Walk with purpose and your attitude will speak volumes to those around you. If at any time you do feel uncomfortable, take some deep, relaxing breaths to release stress, and walk quickly to a safer, busier area. You may also feel happier if you are carrying a personal alarm, or walking a route that you know well

If you are walking in a busy urban area with a high level of traffic, you might want to wear a pollution mask to cut down on inhaling exhaust fumes. This is particularly important for asthma sufferers. To avoid fumes, plan your walks through parks or at less busy times of the day, perhaps before or after rush-hour. When walking somewhere new, make sure you carry a map of the area to avoid getting lost if you veer from the route.

Walking in the dark

When walking at dawn, dusk, or night, make sure you wear reflective stripes on the front and back of your clothing so that you can be seen, and also recognized as a moving body. It is not enough just to wear light clothes. Most shoes, leggings, and jackets now come with luminous stripes, but you can buy them separately if you need to. Buy a fluorescent hat if possible, carry a small torch, and choose walks in well-lit areas.

CHECK LIST TO SAFETY

Your demeanour makes a big difference in avoiding trouble. Look confident and aware, with your head up, and you will appear less vulnerable and not an easy target.

Don't put yourself at risk by ignoring your instincts. If you feel uneasy, act immediately. Move to an area with more people, or go into a shop.

If you are concerned in any way about the area you are planning to walk in, ask a friend to walk with you.

When a stranger is walking towards you, don't look down. Keep your eyes neutral, allow your gaze to rest briefly on the person, then look to either side of the individual. This signals that you are unfazed by his or her presence.

Personal stereos are dangerous when you are walking alone since they prevent you from being alert to your environment. If you really must use one, listen through one earpiece only and keep the volume low.

A personal alarm will make you feel more comfortable when walking alone, even if you never need to use it.

You need to be seen to be safe from traffic – wear reflective strips on the front and back of your clothes.

Carry a little money with you, enough to get you home and provide change for an emergency phone call.

Always carry any information that would be vital in the unlikely event of an accident, such as medical information and contact details for your next of kin.

Try a test walk of your new route in the daylight, or with a friend, to discover if a path is secluded or unsafe.

If you have a mobile phone, store any numbers that you would need in an emergency.

Do not attract attention to yourself – leave your jewellery and valuables at home.

Pack a mini-first aid kit in your bum bag. Essential items include petroleum jelly (to treat chafed skin and sore lips) and plasters or lint-free dressing, just in case.

A map is essential if you are travelling through an unfamiliar area, even if you are following a route.

CARING FOR YOUR BODY

Regular exercise makes you feel great, but don't

forget to spend a little time caring for yourself too.

Treat yourself to a regular pedicure and foot massage,

which will release stress, relax your body, and keep

your feet in good condition. Prevent injuries by

stretching and strengthening vulnerable areas, and act

quickly on minor problems with home treatments

that are simple but effective.

"Life is not merely being alive, but being well."

MARTIAL

BE BODY AWARE

If we take our bodies for granted, we risk ignoring the warning signals they send out in the form of aches and pains when we have overexercised or suffered an injury. In the following pages, you will learn how to diagnose, treat, and prevent some of the most common walking injuries. By listening to your body and adhering to a few rules, you should stay injury-free.

As you begin power walking, you will naturally become more aware of your body, and the effect exercise has on it, both good and bad. Pay attention to your body so that you know how it feels when it is functioning normally. You will then find it easier to recognize an imminent injury, how the stresses of your everyday life are affecting you, or if you are going down with an ailment.

Recognizing the signs

Mild aches and pains are the body's early-warning system. Learn how to read these signs so you can decide whether it is better to rest or train that day. If something is wrong, a self-treatment at home may be all that is required, but if you are in doubt and the pain is severe or chronic, err on the side of caution and consult a doctor.

You may find that as you start power walking, it aggravates an old injury that was not treated properly at the time it occurred. Alternatively, you may discover that you have uncovered a muscular or postural imbalance that was not evident before. In either of these instances, discuss the problem with your doctor.

A useful way of keeping a track of any changes is to keep a log (see pp158–159). Write down the distance you walked and your pace, and alongside it write down how you felt physically and mentally. Plotting any new or unusual aches or pains in diary form will help you to track the cause, and hopefully help you to prevent them reoccurring.

Your support team

Seek out and identify people who can assist you in keeping your body strong and healthy. In my support team, I have my doctor, a chiropractor, a chiropodist, and an acupuncturist. It is sensible to research these people in advance so that you know where to turn to if you do have an injury (see pp154–155).

I would also advise that you visit health specialists for maintenance sessions, not just when you experience pain. Lower back pain is common in power walking, and is usually due to a poor walking posture. Often people lean forwards from the waist with rounded shoulders. The solution is to change your technique, but a visit to the chiropractor on a regular basis acts as a good preventative measure to injury.

Body-scanning

You can use a body-scan meditation to improve your awareness of your body. It teaches you the skill of moving through your body and becoming sensitive to any physical changes.
• Sit comfortably and shake out any tension in your limbs and torso. Take some deep breaths.
• Begin by focusing on the area at the top of your head, then move down over the scalp and forehead, noting any tightness or pressure.
• Move your attention to your face. This is a common area of tension, so check that your eyes are soft and your mouth, tongue, and jaw are relaxed.

• Continue moving down your neck, into your throat, and then into the shoulders, arms, and hands. Again, note any subtle sensations.

• Feel the movement in your ribs and diaphragm with each inhalation and exhalation.

• As you focus on your belly and your lower back, notice your posture and any discomfort.

• Place your awareness on your hips, legs, and feet. Feel your feet firmly planted on the ground. Throughout the scan, breathe normally. If you find an area of tension, keep your awareness there until you feel the knots dissolve away. You may like to repeat the head-to-toe check one or more times, each time going deeper into relaxation.

Checklist for body wellness

Walking is a low-impact sport, so injuries are few and most are preventable, provided you listen to your body and adhere to some simple rules:

Footwear Wear the correct shoes and socks, and possibly orthotics to prevent injury to many parts of the body (*see pp18–23*).

Warm up and cool down Lengthened and warm muscles are less likely to be injured during a walk. Bringing the muscles slowly back into their resting state after exercise is essential (*see pp68–72*).

Stretching and strengthening Stretch every day to ensure your muscles have a full range of motion, and definitely stretch after every walk (*see pp60–72*). Follow a strengthening regime on a daily basis if possible so that your muscles can cope with your training programme (*see pp52–59*).

Rest days Without rest your body will become worn down and unable to repair itself after an intense workout. If you walk fast or for a long distance one day, go slowly or for a shorter walk the next.

Overtraining Being over-ambitious can have a negative effect on your training. Work within your limits and build up your speed and distances slowly, particularly after an injury.

Cross-training When your body is tired from walking, try going for a swim or cycle-ride instead so that you use different muscles (*see pp134–139*).

Change your surface Depending on your injury, it could be that pounding on a hard surface is exacerbating it, so walk slowly on grass or a treadmill for a softer workout (*see pp112–113*).

Take care of your feet Rough skin causes blisters, and these can ruin, or even cancel, a walk (*see pp122–125*).

PEDICURE

A monthly pedicure will give you pretty feet, and help to prevent blisters and bruised toes. Even if you can only spare 20 minutes, make your pedicure as luxurious and as special as you can. To finish, you may like to buff your nails to a natural shine. Add a dot of cocoa butter to each nail, then buff with a soft cloth or a ready-made nail buffer.

YOU WILL NEED

A bowl of warm water • nail clippers • nail file • pumice stone • body moisturizer or foot cream • essential oils • cuticle cream • orange stick • warm towels • thin cotton socks

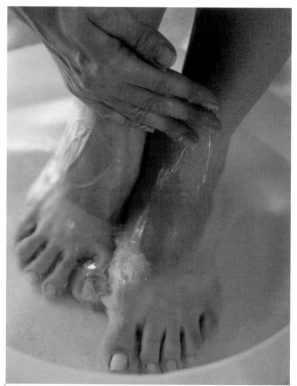

1 Remove rough or hard skin from the foot. This is usually easier to remove when the feet are dry. It tends to form on the heel, ball of the foot, and side of the big toe. When left to build up, it can cause blisters by rubbing on your shoes or socks when you are walking. Use a pumice stone, a dry skin board, or a good foot scrub gently to scrub away hard skin, but don't overdo it.

2 Once you have removed any dry skin, soak your feet in a bowl of warm water for around 5 minutes. Add 2–3 drops of essential oils, such as tea tree (antiseptic), or peppermint (energizing). Lavender essential oil is good for relaxation and balancing, and is one of my favourites.

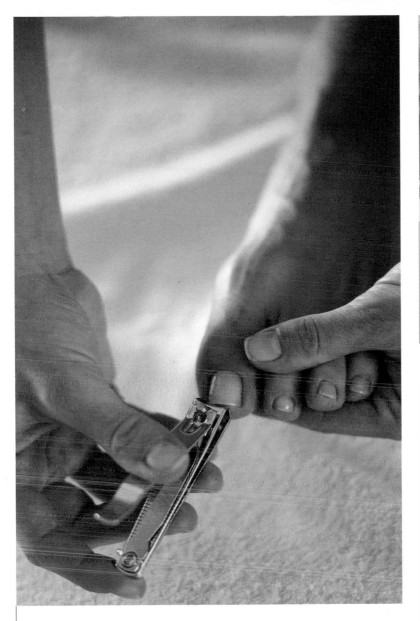

4 Gently massage cuticle cream into the base of each nail and then push back each cuticle with an orange stick. It is better not to cut cuticles as this actually encourages more growth.

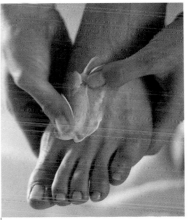

3 Carefully dry your feet, paying special attention between your toes. Clip your toe nails straight across, then use a nail file to smooth along the edge of each nail, stroking lightly in one direction. Make sure that corners are smooth and that there are no sharp edges. It helps to keep your nails short for power walking. If your nails are long, they can hit the toe box of your trainer as you push off, which can lead to bruised toes and black nails (see p128).

5 At this point you might like to give yourself a foot massage (see p124), but if you are short of time, smooth a nourishing body cream or oil into your feet. Put on cotton socks afterwards to allow the moisturizer to soak in.

MASSAGE YOUR FEET

Massaging your feet is a powerful way to ease tension and relax your whole body. There is no time limit, but a minimum of 5–6 repetitions of each movement is much more relaxing than moving onto the next step too quickly. You will need essential oils, a base oil such as almond oil, and two towels.

BE AWARE Always check with a qualified aromatherapist before using any essential oils during pregnancy or if you have a medical condition. Use almond oil on its own if you are unsure.

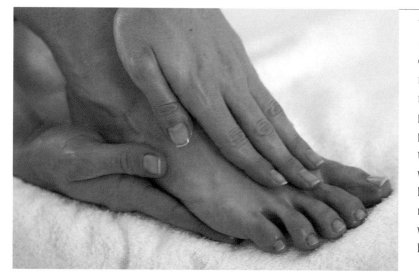

1 Make up a massage oil consisting of 3 drops to 10ml (2 tsp) base oil. A combination of lavender, marjoram, and neroli oils make a very relaxing mix. Prepare your hands by putting a few drops of oil into your palms and massaging your hands together until they feel soft and warm. Hold your foot sandwiched between your hands for a few moments, then stroke your foot with gentle sweeps towards your body, one hand behind the other.

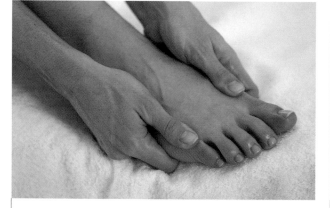

2 Massage each toe using your thumbs. Continue by gliding your thumbs along the top of your foot towards your ankle and then back towards your toes, fanning your thumbs out to the side as you glide.

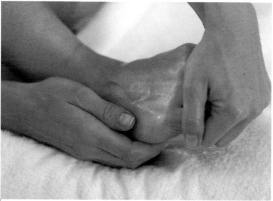

3 Start to loosen your toes by sandwiching them between your palms and rotating them clockwise and then anti-clockwise.

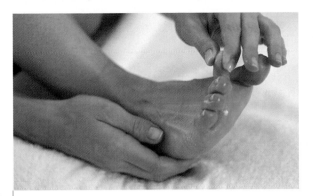

4 Massage each toe again, this time with your thumb and forefinger, give them a light squeeze and a roll. Finally, gently pull each toe in turn towards you.

5 Using gliding movements, run your thumbs between the four tendons on the top of your foot, moving towards the ankle.

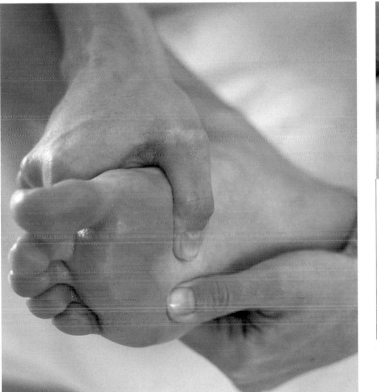

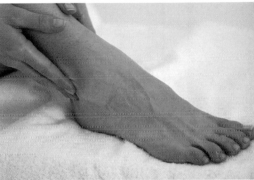

7 Massage around the ankle and Achilles tendon area, making small firm rotations. This feels instantly relaxing as we hold a great deal of tension in our ankles. Complete the massage by stroking the foot. Wrap it in a warm towel or blanket while you work on the other foot.

6 Firmly massage the sole of your foot. Use your thumbs to ease out from the centre to the outer edges. Find a good reflexology book to tell you more about the powerful effect that massaging points on the feet has on the rest of your body.

STAYING INJURY-FREE

By strengthening the parts of the body most used in power walking – notably, the knees, shins, ankles, and hips – you can help to prevent injuries. If you suffer an injury, return to training only once you are fully healed. Even then, the damaged area will be weakened and susceptible to further problems, so when you begin walking again, take it at a slower pace.

Shin splints

Causes and symptoms The calf muscles and the muscles on the front of the shin are probably used more in power walking than in any other sport. The technique (*see pp42–43*) is a distinct way of walking that puts pressure on these muscles to work hard. As a result of this, beginners and over-ambitious experienced walkers can feel a burning, throbbing, or aching sensation, or in milder cases just tenderness, on the front of the shin. Excessive pronation (*see pp18–19*) can also be a cause.

Usually the walker will have been training faster, or for a longer distance, than his or her fitness and ability allows. The muscles are being asked to work in a way they are not used to. A sign of shin splints is that the pain will subside while walking, but will return when you stop.

Treatment and prevention Wrap a bag of frozen peas in a towel and place the ice pack on the shin for around 15 minutes, three times a day, to relieve the muscle ache and inflammation. To relieve the pain and inflammation you can also use a mentholated ointment such as Tiger Balm, an Epsom salt bath, or

an anti-inflammatory. Rest from power walking until you feel comfortable again. When you begin walking, go back a few stages in your training and build up the speed and distance you walk more slowly.

To prevent this injury from recurring, or from appearing to begin with, you need to increase the strength and flexibility in your calf and shin muscles. This can be achieved through regular stretching (*see opposite and p129*). Start stretching the shins and calves gently every day. Also, look into the fit of your shoes, and check they are not too big or too tight, causing your toes to grip.

Sprains and strains

Causes and symptoms A sprain is an injury to a ligament that supports a joint and usually occurs as a result of a fall or a twist. This type of injury can range from first degree, which is a stretching of the ligament, to third degree, the complete separation of the ligament from the bone or even a broken bone. Sprains can take weeks or months to heal.

A strain is an injury to muscles and tendons. These usually come about because of muscle overuse and can range from a minute tear in the muscle to a complete separation of the muscle-tendon-bone attachment.

Both injuries will usually result in painful swelling, inflammation, cramping, and weakness. Sometimes you notice the strain at the time it takes place, or you may notice the pain when you have finished your walk.

> **CAUTION** Any health conditions that you feel may be aggravated through power walking should be discussed with your doctor before you begin. Never ignore serious pain or leave any condition or injury untreated as you may cause irreparable damage. The information on these pages is a guide only. If in any doubt, contact your doctor.

QUAD AND ANKLE STRETCH

This exercise will help to prevent shin splints and sprains and strains (*see opposite*), and plantar fasciitis (*see p130*). Your quads will receive a good stretch and your ankles will be stretched and strengthened as you lift onto your toe. The lift will also strengthen the calves and provide a stretch down the front of the shin.

1 Stand tall in a good posture. If you need to, place one hand on a wall for support. Bend your right leg and, holding your right ankle with your right hand, pull your foot towards your bottom. Keep your knees together and hips square to the front. Tense your buttock muscles to intensify the stretch.

2 Rise up onto the ball of your left foot and hold the position for 4 seconds. Then slowly bring the foot back down to the floor. Repeat the sequence 10 times and then repeat on the opposite leg.

Treatment and prevention The treatment for either of these injuries is to apply the RICE rule: rest, ice, compression, and elevation. Apply an ice pack to the area for 15 minutes, three times a day. Use a wide elastic bandage to wrap up and compress the area, tight enough that you feel some pain relief, but not so tight that the blood supply is cut off. To relieve the pain and inflammation you can also try a mentholated ointment such as Tiger Balm, an Epsom salt bath, or an anti-inflammatory.

Seek professional advice for both conditions because they are painful, they can be serious, and it can be difficult for you to ascertain the degree of injury without a proper examination.

Once the swelling has subsided and the injury is healing, gently begin stretching and strengthening the area (*see p127, p129, p131, and pp52–73*). It is important to keep the area mobile and flexible so that the joints and muscles can heal back to their original strength. When you begin walking, go back a few stages in your training schedule and build up the speed and distance you walk more slowly.

Blisters

Causes and symptoms Blisters are caused by continual rubbing against the skin. A bubble of fluid forms, pocketed between the top layers of skin, and when pressure is applied it feels painful.

Poorly fitting shoes are a common cause of blisters. Socks that are too big, too small, or too old and worn can also result in blisters. Other causes are rough skin or wet feet, either from extreme sweating or walking in rain.

Treatment and prevention The standard advise is to let the fluid subside naturally and if this hasn't happened after 24 hours, to lance the bubble to drain the fluid. I find blisters don't heal quickly unless you lance the bubble immediately. You can sterilize the needle with antiseptic wash, in boiling water, or by heating it in a flame. Pierce two little holes, at either end of the blister. Using sterile gauze, press down gently to remove the liquid.

Wipe the area with an antiseptic solution, and then cover with non-allergenic dressing tape, not lint. This will form a replacement for the skin, allowing the blister to heal in half the time.

If blisters continually return in the same place, make sure that you have the correct shoes for walking and that they fit properly (*see pp18– 23*). If you suspect your socks are the problem (*see p27*), try a different sort. Try covering your feet in petroleum jelly or talcum powder. These act as a barrier and protect the feet from being rubbed. Regular pedicures can also help (*see pp122–123*).

Try a "blister blocker". This is a soft resin that is worked into the skin using your fingers. Make sure you blend the edges so that the resin becomes almost a part of your foot.

Athlete's foot

Causes and symptoms This is a fungus that appears between the toes and on the soles of the feet as cracks of red, flaky, itchy skin that can be quite painful. It can cross-infect from foot-to-nail or nail-to-foot.

Treatment and prevention Apply an anti-fungal (fungicide) cream to the infected areas as directed on the packaging. There are many products available. If athlete's foot returns, as it often does, treat it with a different brand of cream as the fungus may form a tolerance to your usual brand. Continue treating the area for two weeks after the symptoms have disappeared because the fungus can still remain up to this point.

To help prevent a return of the fungus, keep your feet clean and dry at all times. Wear socks made of synthetic fabrics that will wick the moisture from your skin. It is important also to treat your shoes and socks, because washing them is not enough to destroy the fungus.

HEEL-TO-TOE ROCK

This movement helps to prevent shin splints and sprains and strains (*see p126*) by strengthening your shins, calves, and ankles. If you have a weakness in this area, or are a beginner to power walking, this is a very useful move for you to practise. Spend 5 minutes a day on this to enhance your technique.

1 Stand with feet a little less than shoulder-width apart, with your arms and hands hanging loosely by your sides. Legs are straight but knees are soft, and not locked. Bring your weight forwards onto the balls of your feet, using your arms to balance you.

2 Using the momentum of your swing and your arms, rock back onto your heels. Ensure knees remain soft. Repeat the rocking motion 5 times forwards and back, rest for 1 minute, then rock forwards and back a further 5 times.

Black toenails

Causes and symptoms Black toenails are usually caused by shoes that are too small. Each time you push off from your toes as you walk, the toes bang against the end of the toe box in the shoe. Over time this bruises the toes and causes a pooling of blood under the nail, which then blackens. The toe will be painful and will throb under the pressure of the blood that has collected.

Treatment and prevention It is possible to preserve your toenail by lancing it with a sterilized needle through the nail. This is painless, but must be done within an hour of the black toenail appearing. If you don't catch it early enough, or if it isn't too painful, leave it to heal naturally. Over the next few months the nail will fall off, and new nail will have grown underneath. Wear correctly fitting shoes to stop this occurring, and try wearing thicker socks to cushion your toes

Ingrown toenails

Causes and symptoms Ingrown nails occur mostly on the big toe and may be caused by poorly fitting shoes. How you cut and file your toenails may also encourage the toenail to grow into the skin, especially if the toenail is curved or has been cut too short on the sides of the nail. They can be very painful, particularly when the shoe adds pressure to the nail. The skin around the nail will appear red and inflamed, and may become infected.

Treatment and prevention To reduce any swelling and discomfort, soak the affected foot in a bowl of warm water to which you have added 2–4 drops of tea tree essential oil or 1–2 tablespoons of salt at least once a day. If you are unable to cut the nail because it has become embedded in the skin, see a chiropodist, podiatrist, or your doctor.

Always cut toenails in a straight line to prevent the inward growth. Make sure you file any sharp corners with an emery board.

Plantar fasciitis

Causes and symptoms Plantar fasciitis is an inflammation of the plantar fascia, a band of thick tissue that binds the muscle in the sole of the foot, caused by too much stress being placed on the area. It is easy to detect because the pain in your heel will be felt immediately as you get up in the morning or after sitting for some time and then lessens as the day goes on. The pain is often described as feeling like a "bone bruise".

Common causes are continually standing, being overweight, having flat feet (especially if they overpronate, see p18), high arched feet, worn-out shoes which allow overpronation, or a tightness in the Achilles tendon.

Treatment and prevention Rest until the pain disappears. Apply an ice pack to the area for 15–20 minutes four times a day and elevate the foot whenever possible. Healing cannot be rushed, so you may have to be patient.

If you still feel pain after prolonged treatment, visit a chiropodist. You may need heel cups and padding or orthotics (*see p20*) to treat the real problem rather than the symptoms. Roll a small ball underneath your foot, pressing down to get the depth of massage you require. Work on stretching and strengthening the Achilles tendon and calf muscles (*see p129*).Check that your shoes are not too worn and support your arches (*see pp18–23*).

Swollen fingers

Causes and symptoms Fingers swell and become cold when the blood supply is depleted. This can be caused by having your arms and hands down at your sides while walking.

Treatment and prevention Keep your arms at a 90-degree angle (*see pp44–45*) and regularly clench and unclench your fists. By using the correct arm movement, you encourage good blood flow. Wearing gloves also makes a big difference.

BALL SQUATS

This exercise is excellent for preventing strains and sprains (*see p127*). It improves strength and tones up your thighs, hamstrings, buttocks, and quads. Using the ball helps you to put extra weight into your heels, which increases the intensity of the squat. Controlling the ball also gives your lower back a workout.

1 Place the Swiss ball between you and the wall. It should rest behind your lower and middle back. Your knees should be hip-width apart and only slightly bent. Stretch your arms out in front of you to help you balance.

2 Slide slowly down the wall, rolling the ball against it. Stop rolling down when you reach a sitting position with knees bent at a 90 degree angle. Keep your back straight. Hold for 4 counts, then slowly return to the start position. Repeat 5 times, then rest. The slower you do this, the more intense the squat. Increase the number of counts as you grow stronger.

TRAINING PROGRAMMES

Making a commitment to a training programme can feel a little overwhelming, but I hope you will feel excited too. The rewards and satisfaction of sticking to an exercise regime come not just from reaching a goal, but from discovering new strengths and abilities within yourself, and relishing the achievements that you have gained on the way.

"In each of us are places where we have never gone. Only by pressing the limits do you ever find them."
DR JOYCE BROTHERS

CROSS TRAINING

The saying goes, "A change is as good as a rest", and this is certainly true for the body. Power walking works your calves, hamstrings, and glutes particularly hard, so to balance this you need to do activities that work other muscles, or that challenge the same muscles in a different way. Days when you cross train allow your key walking muscles to recover and actually grow stronger.

Any form of exercise is suitable for your cross training, including swimming, cycling, dancing, rollerblading, orienteering, and working out in a gym. Don't feel restricted to this list, though. Any exercise carried out for 30 minutes that raises your heart rate will be beneficial to you.

Swimming

The focus in swimming is on the upper body and torso, and it is therefore excellent cross training for walking. It can give you a good overall cardiovascular workout, though it is not as easy to increase your heart rate as when you are walking. Try building up to 30 minutes of continuous swimming, or try interval training (*see p111*) in the pool.

You might also like to try water-aerobics or pool-walking or -running, which involves walking or running lengths of the pool. This really tones muscle because of the resistance the water creates against your body, making it an excellent way to burn calories.

Cycling

Walking uses the hamstrings and glutes, while riding a bike is good for working the quadriceps, which makes it another excellent cross-training exercise to do with walking. Cycling will keep you aerobically fit, increase your levels of strength and stamina, and support your muscle function. It is a non-impact sport that specifically works the

abductors, which are good for balance and co-ordination.

There are many types of bike available, including those suitable for speed and touring, mountain bikes for off-road trails and orienteering, and racing bikes and tandems. Contact a specialist if you are considering buying a bike to ensure you buy the right one for you. Research different clubs and organizations to discover what type of cycling activity appeals to you.

To benefit fully from the endurance and strength you can gain from cycling you need to be able to cycle for 30 minutes at a sustained speed. It is advisable to work at strengthening your knees, especially if you are going off-road.

Dancing

All types of dancing are suitable for fitness, including salsa, jazz, belly, swing, hip-hop, tango, modern, and old-time. Any of these styles of dance will develop whole body co-ordination because your body is required to move in every direction. Dancing is social, great fun, and a healthy way to get fit.

Depending on the type of dancing and how vigorous you are, it can give you a cardiovascular workout and will certainly put your core stability muscles to the test. Salsa, for example, is excellent for working your abdominal obliques.

Again, depending on your choice of dance, it can be weight bearing and consequently will help to

either strengthen bones or maintain bone density and prevent osteoporosis. Vigorous and sustained dancing for an hour burns approximately 300 calories, which is the same amount as walking or cycling. As with most forms of exercise, to get the maximum benefit you should aim to dance for 30 minutes continuously. As with any vigorous exercise, you should warm up and do some stretches before starting. Cool down and stretch at the end.

Rollerblading

For an activity that can look so effortless, rollerblading burns up a surprisingly large amount of energy, especially when you are learning. It is tremendous for developing core stability and co-ordination, and it particularly works the muscles of the legs and buttocks. Because a lot of your control

Using a variety of swimming strokes will work different muscles and joints. Consider signing up for some swimming classes so that you can improve and develop your technique.

and power comes from the lower body and knees, work at strengthening these muscles with lunges (see p137) and ball squats (see p131).

Orienteering

If you like the excitement of exploring and enjoy being in the countryside, then this is the sport for you (see p103). The routes with their control points are usually through forests and rugged terrains, and vary in lengths from 1.6km (1 mile) for children to 12km (7 miles) for experienced adult orienteers. You can make the workout as hard or easy as you want by running, jogging, or walking. It will test your endurance and give you a whole body workout.

Cycling outdoors is a good sport for reducing stress as most people find it a pleasurable form of exercise, and it is an activity suitable for all ages.

In the gym

Working out in a gym can be a great addition to your fitness programme, particularly on dark winter nights, in bad weather, or if you are recovering from an injury. Most gyms offer a good range of cross-training classes, from kick boxing to Pilates. The variety will help to keep you motivated on your fitness plan. One of the advantages of using equipment such as treadmills and weight machines in a gym is that they are often placed in front of mirrors so that you can continually check and correct your posture. In addition, you have experienced instructors on hand to give advice on using the equipment properly and safely. Use them to pick up exercises that you could do at home and include them in your daily stretch and strengthen routine (*see p73*). I have included here a selection of exercises that can be done at home or in a gym.

The lunge opposite works on strengthening your lower body, and is followed by two excellent exercises for building the muscles in the arms.

Walking on a treadmill

If you are new to using a treadmill, you will find that the display panel offers quite a few readings and programmes to master, such as a calorie counter, heart-rate monitor, speedometer, pace function, and hill walking and terrain programmes. They are easy to use, and your gym instructor will be able to answer any questions.

The sensation of walking on a treadmill is very different to walking on a road, and can feel quite bouncy. This makes walking, jogging, or running easier and faster and puts less strain on your joints. However, a common mistake people make is to walk with the treadmill in a flat position. Although your body is moving forwards with each stride, the treadmill does not require the same level of exertion and muscle power from you as the road does because of the soft surface. In fact, walking flat on a treadmill will eventually lead to weakened muscles. Always set the treadmill to an incline of at least 1 per cent, even as a beginner, to ensure you are replicating your road-walking speed.

Use the heart-rate monitor function to make sure that you match your pace and exertion to that of your road walking. The procedure for stretching, warming up, and cooling down is the same as usual (*see pp68–72*), except that you get off the machine to stretch. Do not walk barefoot on a treadmill – this can be dangerous.

Creating your own hills and terrain on a treadmill can be challenging and fun. The options allow you to build programmes of varying lengths, inclines, and intensity. Moderate-to-steep inclines will give you a good workout, make you a stronger walker, and still offer a low risk of injury. However, inclines of 15 per cent or more will place stress on your shins and ankles and so should not be attempted too often.

Overtraining

Sometimes trying to fit in a walking programme when you have other stresses in your life can lead to overtraining syndrome and burn out. Even if you are not suffering from stress, if you work too hard at your training, and do not take essential rest periods (*see pp120–121*), you may overtrain.

The symptoms of overtraining manifest themselves in different ways in different people, but typically include fatigue, altered sleep patterns, loss of appetite, unquenchable thirst, muscle ache even after a light workout, being depressed or anxious, feeling impatient or easily upset, and having a high resting heart rate. However, you should check that there is no underlying illness that is responsible for the above symptoms.

If you feel you have overtrained, take immediate steps by cutting down on your training. Start keeping a log to monitor your progress, and include details of how you feel both physically and emotionally. Record your sleeping patterns and how restful they are. Treat yourself to a massage or a week's rest. It is easier to prevent overtraining than to recover from it.

LUNGES

These strengthen and tone your quads, hamstrings, calves, and glutes. The abductors and adductors are also used to stabilize you. To increase the challenge, do lunges in bare feet. Weights are optional, but using them will bring faster results. Keep your movements slow and controlled for maximum benefit. Complete 2 sets of 5 lunges on each leg.

1 Check your posture and tighten your abdominals. Take one full stride back with your left foot and land on your toes. Feel equally balanced and on both feet.

2 With your back straight and shoulders relaxed, lunge down to a count of four, bending both knees until they are at 90 degrees. The right knee should not extend over your toes. Hold for 4 counts, then rise to 4 counts.

BICEP CURLS

These curls focus on strengthening and toning the biceps. Doing this exercise regularly will give you great definition in the front of your arms. By doing the curls with one foot on a Swiss ball, you are required to use your balance. At the top of the movement, concentrate on flexing your biceps.

palms up, wrists straight

1 Take one weight in each hand and place your right foot flat on the ball. Focus and stabilize yourself before starting the curls. Check your posture and keep your eyes looking directly ahead. Be aware of your core stability and balance.

2 Hold the weights at right angles to your body. Slowly lift the weights to the count of four. Hold for 4 counts, then slowly come down to a count of 4. Complete 2 sets of 5 curls, then change legs and repeat.

TRICEP DIPS

Here you use your own body weight as resistance instead of free-weights. This exercise is great for toning and strengthening the triceps in the back of the arms. If possible, do tricep dips in the same session as the bicep curls so that both sides of the arms are worked together.

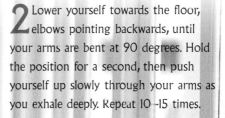

1 Sit on the front edge of a bench or chair. Place your hands by your sides with fingers facing forward. Lift your weight up onto your arms. Arms are straight but elbows are not locked. Keep your knees at 90 degrees and your heels slightly forward from your knees.

2 Lower yourself towards the floor, elbows pointing backwards, until your arms are bent at 90 degrees. Hold the position for a second, then push yourself up slowly through your arms as you exhale deeply. Repeat 10–15 times.

BEGINNER

This programme is designed for anyone who is starting a fitness regime for the very first time, or for people who have not been active for a long period and feel as though they are starting from scratch. The goal is to reach a short-distance walking speed of 1.6km (1 mile) in 15–18 minutes

When starting to power walk it is important to first develop stamina and strength before you deal with speed. Therefore, this programme is split into two halves. Weeks 1 to 6 focus on developing strength, flexibility, and stamina. You will find that as you work on these you will naturally speed up anyway. In weeks 7–12 you will start to develop your speed. Use this programme as a guide that you can adapt to suit your life. It is important to commit yourself to daily activity, so only miss a maximum of one walk a week and never miss a stretching session. Ease yourself slowly into exercise, especially if you are very unfit. Keep a record of your progress using the log on pp158–159. Use the times given here as approximate goals for which you should aim. When you have completed this programme you may wish to try the intermediate programme (pp142–143) or, depending on your ultimate goal, the short-distance programme (pp146–147).

Week 1 Walk 0.8km to 1.6km (½ mile to 1 mile) and decide which distance is the best starting point for you. A steady pace means you do not need to push yourself hard, and can concentrate only on achieving the distance. You may already have more stamina than you think if you are active in your work and around the house. It is more important to get used to the routine of taking exercise than to worry about speed, but no matter how slow you walk try to keep a steady and continuous pace. Stretch for around 5–10 minutes on your rest days to improve your flexibility and strength.

Week 2 Introduce stretching into your walk days as well as your rest days by warming up and cooling down. To warm up, stretch for 5 minutes after the first 10 minutes of your walk, and to cool down, slow your pace about 10 minutes from the end of your walk and stretch immediately after. Start to work on your technique and get used to using your body.

Weeks 3–6 You are walking further and more often, so stretching is vital. From week 4 you should spend 15–20 seconds on each stretch. The other activity you introduce in week 4 can be anything you enjoy, such as swimming or weight-training. Start to work on having different routes to introduce variety and interest to your walks.

Week	Sunday	Monday
1	1.6km (1 mile) at a steady pace	10 mins stretching
2	Rest 10 mins stretching	1.6km (1 mile) at a steady pace
3	1.6km (1 mile) at a steady pace (about 20 mins)	1.6km (1 mile) at a steady pace (about 20 mins)
4	3.2km (2 miles) at a steady pace (about 40 mins)	Rest 15 mins stretching
5	Rest 15 mins Swiss-ball training	3.2km (2 miles) at a steady pace (about 40 mins)
6	3.2km (2 miles) at a steady pace (about 40 mins)	4.8km (3 miles) at a steady pace (about 60 mins)
7	4.8km (3 miles) at a steady pace (about 55 mins)	3.2km (2 miles) at a faster pace (about 35 mins)
8	3.2km (2 miles) at a faster pace (about 35 mins)	3.2km (2 miles) at a faster pace (about 35 mins)
9	3.2km (2 miles) at a faster pace (30–34 mins)	4.8km (3 miles) at a steady pace (about 51 mins)
10	4.8km (3 miles) at a faster pace (about 50 mins)	4.8km (3 miles) at a faster pace (about 50 mins)
11	4.8km (3 miles) at a faster pace (45–50 mins)	4.8km (3 miles) at a faster pace (45–50 mins)
12	6.4km (4 miles) at a steady pace (about 68 mins)	4.8km (3 miles) at speed (about 45 mins)

Exercise Pages • Stretching exercises pp60–67 • Warming up and cooling down, see Warm-up and Cool-down sequences p72 • Swiss-ball training, see pp56–59, p131, p139

Tuesday	Wednesday	Thursday	Friday	Saturday	Total km (miles)
1.6km (1 mile) at a steady pace	Rest 10 mins stretching	1.6km (1 mile) at a steady pace	Rest 10 mins stretching	1.6km (1 mile) at a steady pace	6.4km (4 miles)
Rest 10 mins stretching	1.6km (1 mile) at a steady pace	Rest 10 mins stretching	1.6km (1 mile) at a steady pace	Rest 10 mins stretching	4.8km (3 miles)
1.6km (1 mile) at a steady pace (about 20 mins)	Rest 10 mins stretching	1.6km (1 mile) at a steady pace (about 20 mins)	1.6km (1 mile) at a steady pace (about 20 mins)	1.6km (1 mile) at a steady pace (about 20 mins)	9.6km (6 miles)
3.2km (2 miles) at a steady pace (about 40 mins)	3.2km (2 miles) at a steady pace (about 40 mins)	10 mins stretching	any other activity for a minimum of 15 mins	10 mins stretching	9.6km (6 miles)
Rest 15 mins Swiss-ball training	any other activity for a minimum 30 mins	4.8km (3 miles) at a steady pace (about 60 mins)	Rest 15 mins Swiss-ball training	3.2km (2 miles) at a steady pace (about 40 mins)	11.2km (7 miles)
Rest 15 mins stretching	any other activity for a minimum of 30 mins	3.2km (2 miles) at a steady pace (about 40 mins)	3.2km (2 miles) at a steady pace (about 40 mins)	3.2km (2 miles) at a steady pace (about 40 mins)	17.6km (11 miles)
any other activity for a minimum of 30 mins	Rest 15 mins stretching	4.8km (3 miles) at a steady pace (about 55 mins)	3.2km (2 miles) at a faster pace (about 35 mins)	1.6km (1 mile) at speed (about 18 mins)	17.6km (11 miles)
3.2km (2 miles) at a faster pace (about 32 mins)	4.8km (3 miles) at a steady pace (about 50 mins)	any other activity for a minimum of 15 mins	Rest 15 mins stretching	3.2km (2 miles) at a faster pace (about 32 mins)	17.6km (11 miles)
any other activity for a minimum of 30 mins	3.2km (2 miles) at a faster pace (30–34 mins)	4.8km (3 miles) at a faster pace (about 48 mins)	Rest 15 mins Swiss-ball training	3.2km (2 miles) at a faster pace (30–34 mins)	19.2km (12 miles)
Rest 15 mins stretching	any other activity for a minimum of 30 mins	3.2km (2 miles) at speed (about 30 mins)	4.8km (3 miles) at a faster pace (about 50 mins)	4.8km (3 miles) at a faster pace (about 50 mins)	22.4km (14 miles)
Rest 15 mins stretching	any other activity for a minimum of 30 mins	4.8km (3 miles) at a faster pace (45–50 mins)	4.8km (3 miles) at a faster pace (45–50 mins)	4.8km (3 miles) at a faster pace (45–50 mins)	24km (15 miles)
any other activity for a minimum of 30 mins	6.4km (4 miles) at a steady pace (70–98 mins)	4.8km (3 miles) at speed (45–50 mins)	Rest 15 mins stretching	6.4km (4 miles) at speed (about 60 mins)	28.8km (18 miles)

Week 7 As you begin moving at a faster pace, you are working on strength and developing technique. At a faster pace you are walking with purpose, and should feel that you are exerting yourself, but you should still be able to talk as you walk. If you do not feel ready for this, go back to week 5 and complete the last two weeks again. If you feel fine then continue into week 7.

Weeks 8–12 Walking at speed means you need to work harder and push forwards a little more. Listen to your body and if you find the pace is too hard, take it down a notch. If you wish, you can introduce interval training.

Other pages that will help you • Using the Borg scale, see pp32–35 • Setting your stride pp36–37 • Any other activity, see pp134–137 • Interval training, see pp110–111 • Walking log pp158–159

INTERMEDIATE

If you are able to walk 6.4km (4 miles) at a constant pace and want to take the next step in training, then you are ready for the intermediate programme. Exercising and stretching on a daily basis will keep you fit, strengthen your body, make you leaner and more toned, and develop your speed and walking technique.

To achieve results, you must be prepared to walk 3–4 times a week. Use this programme as a guide to plan a training schedule that fits your life. Daily stretching and strengthening are important parts of the programme and will make a big difference to your flexibility and strength, allowing you to progress more rapidly. It takes the body 4–6 weeks to get used to a new cardiovascular pattern and it is better not to work on stamina and speed simultaneously. You will find that they eventually do come together during the course of the programme. Use the times given here as approximate goals for which you should aim. Always follow a hard training day by an easier one.

Weeks 1–3 First you must develop your strength and stamina by walking longer distances at a constant pace. Introduce stretching before and after every walk, using the warm-up and cool-down programmes. To warm up, stretch for 5 minutes after the first 10 minutes of your walk, and to cool down, slow your pace about 10 minutes from the end and finish with 10 minutes stretching. From the first day you will need to do stretching and strengthening exercises for around 15 minutes a day. The other activity mentioned in the programme is your own choice and can be anything you enjoy, such as swimming or cycling. Interval training is a good way to add variety to your walks. This works the body quite hard, so have a rest day afterwards or an easy walk.

Weeks 4–5 Where hill walking is specified, this is optional, but walking routes that take you up and down hills are an excellent way to build strength and stamina. Core stability sessions are introduced in week 4 and vary in duration, the first lasts 30 minutes. Use a pedometer to plot your progress, and keep a log using the template on pp158–159.

Weeks 6–12 You are now developing stamina, strength, and technique. Increase your speed in these weeks. Vary your pace, pushing hard on some days, and easing off on others. Now, stepping up a gear, you may want to start using a heart rate monitor to track your progress and assist your training.

Week	Sunday	Monday
1	4.8km (3 miles) (45–55 mins) + 15 mins stretch and strengthen	any other activity for 30 minutes
2	6.4km (4 miles) (about 60–68 mins) + 15 mins stretch and strengthen	Rest 15 mins stretch and strengthen
3	Rest 15 mins stretch and strengthen	4.8km (3 miles) (45–55 mins) + 15 mins stretch and strengthen
4	30 mins core stability training	9.6km (6 miles) (90–100 mins) + 15 mins stretch and strengthen
5	Rest 15 mins stretch and strengthen	11.2km (7 miles) (105–112 mins) + 15 mins stretch and strengthen
6	12.9km (8 miles) (120–128 mins) + 15 mins stretch and strengthen	Rest 15 mins stretch and strengthen
7	14.4km (9 miles) (135–144 mins) + 15 mins stretch and strengthen	Rest 15 mins stretch and strengthen
8	Rest 15 mins stretch and strengthen	8km (5 miles) (about 75 mins) + 15 mins stretch and strengthen
9	any other activity for a minimum of 30 mins	Rest 15 mins stretch and strengthen
10	16km (10 miles) (about 150 mins) + 15 mins stretch and strengthen	Rest 15 mins stretch and strengthen
11	Rest 15 mins stretch and strengthen	8km (5 miles) (about 70–75 mins) + 15 mins stretch and strengthen
12	6.4km (4 miles) hill walking (about 60 mins) + 15 mins stretch and strengthen	Rest 15 mins stretch and strengthen

Exercise pages • Warming up and cooling down, see Warm-up and Cool-down plans p72 • Stretch and strengthen, see Stretching and Strengthening plan p73 • Core stability training, see pp54–59

Tuesday	Wednesday	Thursday	Friday	Saturday	Total km (miles)
Rest 15 mins stretch and strengthen	4.8km (3 miles) (45–55 mins) + 15 mins stretch and strengthen	Rest 15 mins stretch and strengthen	4.8km (3 miles) (45–55 mins) + 15 mins stretch and strengthen	Rest 15 mins stretch and strengthen	14.4km (9 miles)
4.8km (3 miles) (45–55 mins) + 15 mins stretch and strengthen	Rest 15 mins stretch and strengthen	any other activity for a minimum of 15 minutes	Rest 15 mins stretch and strengthen	6.4km (4 miles) (60–68 mins) + 15 mins stretch and strengthen	17.6km (11 miles)
4.8km (3 miles) hill walking (50–55 mins) + 15 mins stretch and strengthen	Rest 15 mins stretch and strengthen	any other activity for a minimum of 30 minutes	8.1km (5 miles) (75–80 mins) + 15 mins stretch and strengthen	Rest 15 mins stretch and strengthen	17.6k (11 miles)
Rest 15 mins stretch and strengthen	8km (5 miles) (75–80 mins) + 15 mins stretch and strengthen	Rest 15 mins stretch and strengthen	4.8km (3 miles) (45–50 mins) + 15 mins stretch and strengthen	any other activity for a minimum of 30 minutes	22.4km (14 miles)
Rest 15 mins stretch and strengthen	9.6km (6 miles) (90–96 mins) + 15 mins stretch and strengthen	Rest 30 mins core stability training	Rest 15 mins stretch and strengthen	6.4km (4 miles) (60–64 mins) + 15 mins stretch and strengthen	27.2km (17 miles)
9.6km (6 miles) (about 90 mins) + 15 mins stretch and strengthen	4.8km (3 miles) interval training (45–50 mins) + 15 mins stretch and strengthen	Rest 15 mins stretch and strengthen	any other activity for a minimum of 30 mins	6.4km (4 miles) (about 60 mins) + 15 mins stretch and strengthen	33.7km (21 miles)
8km (5 miles) (75–80 mins) + 15 mins stretch and strengthen	any other activity for a minimum of 30 mins	Rest 15 mins stretch and strengthen	4.8km (3 miles) interval training (about 45 mins) + 15 mins stretch and strengthen	11.2km (7 miles) (about 105 mins) + 15 mins stretch and strengthen	38.4km (24 miles)
4.8km (3 miles) hill walking (42–48 mins) 15 mins stretch and strengthen	Rest 15 mins stretch and strengthen	6.4km (4 miles) (56–60 mins) + 15 mins stretch and strengthen	Rest 15 mins stretch and strengthen	14.4km (9 miles) (135–140 mins) + 15 mins stretch and strengthen	33.7km (21 miles)
4.8km (3 miles) interval training (about 45 mins) + 15 mins stretch and strengthen	Rest 15 mins stretch and strengthen	8km (5 miles) (70–75 mins) + 15 mins stretch and strengthen	6.4km (4 miles) (56–60 mins) + 15 mins stretch and strengthen	Rest 15 mins stretch and strengthen	19.2km (12 miles)
6.4km (4 miles) interval training (58–60 mins) + 15 mins stretch and strengthen	6.4km (4 miles) (about 60 mins) + 15 mins stretch and strengthen	Rest 15 mins stretch and strengthen	any other activity for 60 mins	11.2km (7 miles) (about 98 mins) + 15 mins stretch and strengthen	40km (25 miles)
Rest 15 mins stretch and strengthen	6.4km (4 miles) interval training (55–60 mins) + 15 mins stretch and strengthen	Rest 15 mins stretch and strengthen	any other activity for 60 mins	14.4km (9 miles) (126–135 mins) + 15 mins stretch and strengthen	28.8km (18 miles)
9.6km (6 miles) (84–90 mins) + 15 mins stretch and strengthen	60 mins core stability training	4.8km (3 miles) (39–42 mins) + 15 mins stretch and strengthen	Rest 15 mins stretch and strengthen	16km (10 miles) (140–150 mins) + 15 mins stretch and strengthen	36.8km (23 miles)

Other pages that will help you • Using a heart rate monitor, see pp32–35 • Any other activity, see pp134–137 • Hill walking, see pp112–113 • Using a pedometer, see pp36–37 • Interval training, see pp110–111 • Foods for fitness pp90–91 • Fit walking into your day pp94–95

ADVANCED

This programme is for walkers who wish to increase intensity and distance to their walking. There are three stages to the programme: the first builds stamina, the second focuses on speed, and the third works on stamina and speed together to help you achieve a high level of ability. Your aim at the end of the programme is to walk 11–12 minutes per 1.6km (1 mile).

Before you start this programme you must be able to walk 1.6km (1 mile) in 15 minutes at a constant pace, and walk comfortably for 16km (10 miles) at a reasonable pace. You can return to any part of this programme at any time and repeat weeks until you are ready to move on to the next stage. This programme sets you both a distance to walk and an ideal speed in which to complete it. If you walk to the speed suggested for each kilometre (or mile) you will progress quickly. However, always match the intensity of your walk to what you feel you can manage on a given day. A training walk can be exchanged for working with weights for 30 minutes or a walk on a treadmill if you wish, but not more than once a week. Adapt the programme to suit your ability by using a heart rate monitor to ensure you work at your peak. Add interest to your walks by using interval training combined with a heart rate monitor. If time is short, concentrate on short distances and vary your speeds, or do interval training. When you have completed the 12 weeks, use the table as a guide and increase distance and speed as required.

Week 1–4 In these weeks you are building stamina and strength with daily stretching, core stability exercises, and long distance walking. Warm up and cool down for each walk. Stretching and strengthening is important because it helps you to walk at speed. To make the sequence fit the time specified, hold stretches for longer and include more repetitions on other exercises. Interval training is a good way to add variety to your walks. It does work the body quite hard, so have a rest day afterwards or an easy walk. To add variety to your walks, you have the option of hill walking from Week 3 onwards. This means walking a route that takes you up and down hills.

Week 5–8 The focus is now on shorter distances but with intensity and speed. You should stay away from uneven ground, and keep to roads and pavements for these walks.

Week 9–12 You are now walking both longer distances and in a shorter time. Make sure that you have a good mixture of routes and different terrains to keep you motivated.

Week	Sunday	Monday
1	6.4 x 10-minute km (4 x 15-minute miles) (about 60 mins)	60 mins core stability training
2	Rest 30 mins stretch and strengthen	9.6 x 8–9-minute km (6 x 15-minute miles) (about 90 mins)
3	Rest 30 mins stretch and strengthen	8 x 10–11-minute km (5 x 14–15-minute miles) (about 70 mins) + 15 mins stretch and strengthen
4	19.2 x 10-minute km (12 x 15-minute miles) (about 180 mins) + 20 mins stretch and strengthen	any other activity for 30 mins
5	4.8 x 10-minute km (3 x 14-minute miles) (about 42 mins)	6.4 x 7–8-minute km (4 x 12–13-minute miles) interval training (44–52 mins)
6	4.8 x 9–10-minute km (3 x 13–14-minute miles) (39–42 mins)	6.4 x 7–8-minute km (4 x 11–13-minute miles) interval training (44–52 mins)
7	6.4 x 10-minute km (4 x 15-minute miles) (about 60 mins)	9.6 x 8–9-minute km (6 x 13–14-minute miles) (78–84 mins)
8	3.2 x 8–9-minute km (2 x 13–14 minute miles) (26–28 mins)	4.8 x 10-minute km (3 x 15-minute miles) (about 45 mins)
9	any other activity for 30 mins	6.4km (4 miles) interval training (48–54 mins)
10	8 x 9-minute km (5 x 14-minute miles) (about 70 mins) + 20 mins core stability training	11.2 x 8–9-minute km (7 x 12–14-minute miles) (84–98 mins)
11	19.2 x 8–10-minute km (12 x 13–14-minute miles) (156–168 mins) + 20 mins stretch and strengthen	30 mins core stability training
12	6.4 x 10-minute km (4 x 15-minute miles) (about 60 mins)	8 x 7–8-minute km (5 x 11–13-minute miles) (55–65 mins) + 15 mins stretch and strengthen

Exercise pages • Warming up and cooling down, see Warm-up and Cool-down plan p72 • Core Stability training, see pp54-59 • Stretch and strengthen, see Stretching and strengthening plan p73 • Swiss-ball training, see pp56-59, p131, p139

Tuesday	Wednesday	Thursday	Friday	Saturday	Total km (miles)
8 x 10-minute km (5 x 15-minute miles) (about 75 mins) + 15 mins stretch and strengthen	Rest 30 mins stretch and strengthen	9.6 x 10-minute km (6 x 15-minute miles) (about 90 mins)	any other activity for 30 mins minimum	16 x 10-minute km (10 x 15-minute miles) (about 150 mins)	40km (25 miles)
any other activity for 60 mins	11.2 x 8–9-minute km (7 x 15-minute miles) (about 105 mins)	6.4km (4 miles) interval training (about 56 mins)	8 x 10-minute km (5 x 15-minute miles) (about 75 mins) + 20 mins stretch and strengthen	19.2 x 10-minute km (12 x 15-minute miles) (about 180 mins)	54.4km (34 miles)
11.2 x 10-minute km (7 x 15-minute miles) hill walking (105 mins)	any other activity for 60 mins	11.2 x 9–10-minute km (7 x 14–15-minute miles) (98–105 mins) + 15 mins stretch and strengthen	8 x 8–9-minute km (5 x 13–14-minute miles) (65–70 mins)+ 20 mins stretch and strengthen	30 mins Swiss-ball training	38.4km (24 miles)
8 x 10-minute km (5 x 15-minute miles) (about 75 mins)	11.2 x 8–9-minute km (7 x 13–14-minute miles) (91–98 mins)	9.6km (6 miles) hill walking (about 90 mins)	11.2 x 10-minute km (7 x 15-minute miles) (about 105 mins)+ 20 mins stretch and strengthen	30 mins Swiss-ball training	59.2km (37 miles)
3.2 x 10-minute km (2 x 15-minute miles) (about 30 mins)	3.2 x 9–10-minute km (2 x 13–14-minute miles) (26–28 mins)	30 mins core stability training	6.4 x 7–8-minute km (4 x 11–13-minute miles) interval training (44–52 mins)	8 x 10-minute km (5 x 15-minute miles) (about 75 mins)	32km (20 miles)
30 mins core stability training	9.6 x 10-minute km (6 x 15-minute miles) (about 90 mins)	6.4 x 7–8-minute km (4 x 11–13-minute miles) (44–52 mins)	8 x 10-minute km (5 x 15 minute miles) (about 75 mins)	4.8 x 9–10-minute km (3 x 13–14-minute miles) (39–42 mins)	40km (25 miles)
3.2 x 7–8-minute km (2 x 11–13-minute miles) interval training (22–26 mins)	8 x 10-minute km (5 x 15-minute miles) (about 75 mins)	30 mins core stability training	6.4 x 8–9-minute km (3 x 11–13-minute miles) (33–39 mins)	4.8 x 7–8-minute km (3 x 11–13-minute miles) (33–39 mins)	38.4km (23 miles)
6.4 x 7–8-minute km (4 x 11–13-minute miles) (44–52 mins)	30 mins core stability training	3.2 x 10-minute km (2 x 13-minute miles) interval training (about 26 mins)	4.8 x 10-minute km (3 x 15-minute miles) (about 45 mins)	6.4 x 7–8-minute km (4 x 11–13-minute miles) (44–52 mins)	28.8km (18 miles)
9.6 x 7–8-minute km (6 x 11–13-minute miles) (66–78 mins)	30 mins core stability training	4.8 x 8-minute km (3 x 12-minute miles) (about 36 mins)	6.4km (4 miles) hill walking (52–60 mins)	16 x 9–10-minute km (10 x 13–15 minute miles) (130–150 mins)	43.2km (27 miles)
30 mins core stability training	any other activity for 60 mins	6.4km (4 miles) hill walking (48–52 mins) + 15 mins stretch and strengthen	9.6km (6 miles) interval training (78–84 mins) + 20 mins stretch and strengthen	11.2 x 7–9-minute km (7 x 12–14-minute miles) (84–98 mins) + 15 mins stretch and strengthen	46.4km (29 miles)
4.8 x 7-minute km (3 x 11-minute miles) (about 33 mins) + 20 mins stretch and strengthen	8 x 9-minute km (5 x 14-minute miles) (about 70 mins) + 15 mins stretch and strengthen	any other activity for 30 mins	9.6 x 8-minute km (6 x 11–13-minute miles) (66–78 mins) 20 mins stretch and strengthen	16 x 8–9-minute km (10 x 13–14-minute miles) hill walking (130–140 mins)	57.6km (36 miles)
any other activity for 60 mins	4.8 km (3 miles) interval training (33–39 mins)	30 mins core stability training	8 x 10-minute km (5 x 15-minute miles) (about 75 mins) + 15 mins stretch and strengthen	19.2 x 7–8-minute km (12 x 11–13-minute miles) (132–143 mins)	46.4km (29 miles)

Other pages to help you • Using a heart rate monitor, see pp32-35 • Any other activity, see pp134-137 • Interval training, see pp110–111 • Hill walking, see pp112-113 • Staying injury-free pp126-131 • Foods for fitness pp90–91

SHORT DISTANCE

The aim of this programme is to help you reach a level of fitness that allows you to power walk for one hour a day. Before you begin, you must be able to walk for 15 minutes at any speed. If this is uncomfortable for you, try the beginner programme (pp140–141) until you reach this level of ability.

As a guide, 1.6km (1 mile) in 15 minute is a good pace for you to aim at. The average person walks 2.4–4.8km (2½–3 miles) per hour and your aim by the end of this 12-week programme is to walk at 6.4km (about 4 miles) per hour. This table is based on minutes walked not distance. By completing short distances regularly, your stamina and speed will increase simultaneously. Success is guaranteed if you power walk at least four times a week and exert yourself for the specified period of time. Daily walks of a minimum of 30 minutes could be split into two 15-minute walks so that the programme can fit your life more easily.

Use the log on pp158–159 to record your routes and speeds; the comments box is to note whatever you experience as you walk through the seasons. Use a pedometer to see how much further you go in the same amount of time as you progress.

Week 1 Start with a steady pace, speed is not important. Allow your body to adapt to the idea of walking every day and notice how your body feels. Warm up before each walk by stretching 5 minutes into the beginning of your walk, and cool down by slowing for the last 10 minutes of your walk and stretching immediately after. Reduce the amount of time on warm-up and cool-down stretches on shorter walks of 30 minutes or less.

Week 2 If you are ready, use more exertion. You should feel that your body is working harder (a heart rate monitor will give you a more accurate measurement of how hard), but you should be able to talk as you walk.

Week 3 By now you should feel you have more energy and if you are comfortable with the length of time you are walking, start to increase your speed further.

Weeks 4–12 From this point on, increase your speed if you can. Try interval training for variety in your walks. Interval training does work the body quite hard, so don't interval train two days in a row.

Week	Sunday	Monday
1	15 minutes	15 minutes
2	20 minutes	15 minutes
3	20 minutes	15 minutes
4	20 minutes	25 minutes
5	20 minutes	20 minutes
6	25 minutes	30 minutes
7	25 minutes	30 minutes
8	30 minutes	35 minutes
9	30 minutes	40 minutes
10	30 Minutes	40 minutes
11	30 minutes	40 minutes
12	40 minutes	50 minutes

Exercise pages • Warming up and cooling down, see Warm-up and Cool-down plans p72 • Stretching and strengthening plan p73

Tuesday	Wednesday	Thursday	Friday	Saturday	Total minutes
15 minutes	20 minutes	15 minutes	15 minutes	15 minutes	110 minutes
20 minutes	15 minutes	15 minutes	15 minutes	15 minutes	115 minutes
20 minutes	20 minutes	15 minutes	25 minutes	20 minutes	135 minutes
20 minutes	20 minutes	25 minutes	25 minutes	30 minutes	165 minutes
25 minutes	30 minutes	20 minutes	25 minutes	30 minutes	170 minutes
30 minutes	25 minutes	30 minutes	30 minutes	35 minutes	205 minutes
40 minutes	25 minutes	30 minutes	40 minutes	40 minutes	230 minutes
40 minutes	30 minutes	35 minutes	40 minutes	40 minutes	250 minutes
40 minutes	30 minutes	30 minutes	30 minutes	50 minutes	250 minutes
50 minutes	30 minutes	40 minutes	40 minutes	50 minutes	280 minutes
50 minutes	30 minutes	30 minutes	50 minutes	60 minutes	290 minutes
60 minutes	30 minutes	40 minutes	50 minutes	60 minutes	330 minutes

Other pages to help you • Using a pedometer, see pp36–37 • Using a heart rate monitor, see pp32–35 • Interval training, see pp110–111 • Walking log pp158–159 • Posture and breathing pp40–41 • Fit walking into your day pp94–95

HALF MARATHON

To begin this programme you must be able to walk 3.2km (2 miles) at a constant speed of approximately 18–20 minutes per 1.6km (1 mile). If you are unable to do this, try the beginner programme (pp140–141) until you are able to achieve this pace. By the end of the half-marathon programme, your aim is to be walking at a speed of 14–15 minutes per 1.6km (1 mile). A good finishing time for a half marathon is 2¾–3 hours

Use this programme as a guide only and adapt it to suit your level of fitness and your life. The goal is to achieve a good, constantly maintained speed over 21.1km (13.2 miles), the distance of a half marathon. The programme starts with walks at a steady pace over longer distances to build stamina and strength. When you feel ready, pick up the pace to work on your speed. Use the times given here as approximate goals for which you should aim. It takes 4–6 weeks for your body to fully adapt to any cardiovascular change – too fast too soon can cause injuries. Eventually, you will find that speed and stamina will come together.

Weeks 1–2 Start with a steady pace and pay particular attention to your posture and technique. A steady pace means you do not need to push yourself hard. Warm up before each walk by stretching 5 minutes into the beginning of your walk, and cool down by slowing for the last 10 minutes of your walk and stretching immediately after. On your rest days, stretch and strengthen for at least 10 minutes, or longer if you would prefer, using the daily stretching and strengthening plan.

Week 3 Any other activity can be anything you choose for a minimum of 15 minutes that increases your heart rate, such as swimming, dancing, or rollerblading. You are now walking at a faster pace, which means you are walking with purpose and that you are exerting yourself, but you should still able to talk as you walk.

Weeks 4–12 Start to exert yourself a little more on your short walks and maintain a constant speed. Your rest and stretch days are as important as your walking days. Walking at speed means that you need to work a little harder and are pushing forwards more. You must complete a walk of at least 16km (10 miles) no less than two weeks before the actual event, not least because it will mentally prepare you for the walk itself.

Week	Sunday	Monday
1	3.2km (2 miles) at a steady pace (about 40 mins)	Rest 10–15 mins stretch and strengthen
2	Rest 10–15 mins stretch and strengthen	3.2km (2 miles) at a steady pace (about 36 mins)
3	Rest 10–15 mins stretch and strengthen	4.8km (3 miles) at a faster pace (about 54 mins)
4	Rest 10–15 mins stretch and strengthen	4.8km (3 miles) at a faster pace (about 54 mins)
5	9.6km (6 miles) at a steady pace (about 105 mins)	Rest 10–15 mins stretch and strengthen
6	9.6km (6 miles) at a steady pace (about 96 mins)	any other activity for a minimum of 30 mins
7	11.2km (7 miles) at a steady pace (about 115 mins)	Rest 10–15 mins stretch and strengthen
8	any other activity for a minimum of 30 mins	4.8km (3 miles) at speed (about 42 mins)
9	12.9km (8 miles) at speed (about 120 mins)	Rest 10–15 mins stretch and strengthen
10	Rest 10–15 mins stretch and strengthen	any other activity for a minimum of 30 mins
11	16km (10 miles) at speed (about 140 mins)	Rest 10–15 mins stretch and strengthen
12	Rest; 10–15 mins stretch and strengthen	any other activity for a minimum of 30 mins

Exercise pages • Warming up and cooling down, see Warm-up and cool-down plan p72 • Stretch and strengthen, see Stretching and strengthening plan p73

Tuesday	Wednesday	Thursday	Friday	Saturday	Total km (miles)
3.2km (2 miles) at a steady pace (about 40 mins)	Rest 10–15 mins stretch and strengthen	3.2km (2 miles) at a steady pace (about 40 mins)	Rest 10–15 mins stretch and strengthen	4.8km (3 miles) at a steady pace (about 60 mins)	14.4km (9 miles)
Rest 10–15 mins stretch and strengthen	4.8km (3miles) at a steady pace (about 54 mins)	Rest 10–15 mins stretch and strengthen	Rest 10–15 mins stretch and strengthen	4.8km (3miles) at a steady pace (about 54 mins)	12.8km (8 miles)
any other activity for a minimum of 30 mins	6.4km (4 miles) at a steady pace (about 80 mins)	Rest 10–15 mins stretch and strengthen	any other activity for a minimum of 30 mins	8km (5 miles) at a steady pace (about 100 mins)	19.2km (12 miles)
any other activity for a minimum of 30 mins	4.8km (3miles) at a faster pace (about 50 mins)	Rest 10–15 mins stretch and strengthen	4.8km (3miles) at a faster pace (about 50 mins)	Rest 10–15 mins stretch and strengthen	14.4km (9 miles)
4.8km (3 miles) at speed (about 48 mins)	any other activity for a minimum of 30 mins	6.4km (4 miles) at speed (60–64 mins)	Rest 10–15 mins stretch and strengthen	any other activity for a minimum of 30 mins	20.8km (13 miles)
6.4km (4 miles) at speed (about 60 mins)	Rest 10–15 mins stretch and strengthen	6.4km (4 miles) at speed (about 60 mins)	any other activity for a minimum of 30 mins	Rest 10–15 mins stretch and strengthen	22.4km (14 miles)
6.4km (4 miles) at speed (about 56 mins)	Rest 10–15 mins stretch and strengthen	6.4km (4 miles) at speed (about 56 mins)	Rest 10–15 mins stretch and strengthen	8km (5 miles) at a steady pace (about 80 mins)	32km (20 miles)
any other activity for a minimum of 30 mins	4.8km (3 miles) at speed (about 42 mins)	any other activity for a minimum of 30 mins	4.8km (3 miles) at speed (about 42 mins)	Rest 10–15 mins stretch and strengthen	14.4km (9 miles)
6.4km (4 miles) at speed (56–60 mins)	Rest 10–15 mins stretch and strengthen	6.4km (4 miles) at speed (56–60 mins)	any other activity for a minimum of 30 mins	12.9km (8 miles) at speed (about 112 mins)	38.6km (24 miles)
6.4km (4 miles) at speed (about 55–60 mins)	Rest 10–15 mins stretch and strengthen	6.4km (4 miles) at speed (55–60 mins)	any other activity for a minimum of 30 mins	Rest 10–15 mins stretch and strengthen	12.8km (8 miles)
Rest 10–15 mins stretch and strengthen	4.8km (3 miles) at speed (40–43 mins)	any other activity for a minimum of 30 mins	Rest 10–15 mins stretch and strengthen	4.8km (3 miles) at speed (40–43 mins)	25.6km (16 miles)
Rest; 10–15 mins stretch and strengthen	4.8km (3 miles) at speed (about 40 mins)	Rest; 10–15 mins stretch and strengthen	4.8km (3 miles) at speed (about 40 mins)	Rest; 10–15 mins stretch and strengthen	9.6km (6 miles)

Other pages to help you • Foods for fitness pp90–91 • Preparing for a marathon, see pp106–107 • Using a heart rate monitor, see pp32–35 • Any other activity, see pp134–137

MARATHON

Marathons are walked for many reasons, from beating a personal best time to raising money for charity, but everyone wants to cross the finish line. Follow this 12-week programme and you should have no problems on the day. It is vital that as part of your training you complete at least one walk of about 32km (20 miles). A good finishing time for a marathon (42.2km/26¼ miles) is 6 hours. The aim is to walk at a speed of 12–14 minutes per 1.6 km (1 mile).

For this programme you must be able to walk 4.8km (3 miles) at a steady speed of approximately 18–20 minutes per 1.6 km (1 mile). If you are unable to do this, follow the beginner programme until you can achieve this pace, then return to this programme. If you need to train on a treadmill because of time restraints or lack of daylight hours, ensure that at least 50 per cent of your training is on roads. Use the times given here as approximate goals for which you should aim.

Weeks 1–2 Work on your technique and posture in these first weeks and walk at a comfortable and constant pace, but make sure that you can feel an increase in your heart rate and that you are exerting yourself beyond your normal pace. However, going too fast too soon can cause injuries, so focus on a constant pace over speed. Warm up and cool down for each walk. On the days when you are not walking, set aside time for stretching and strengthening. Start with a session of around 10 minutes and extend this as time goes on.

Week 3 You need to be walking at a faster pace now, which means exerting yourself, but ensure you are still able to talk as you walk. The other activity can be anything you enjoy, such as swimming, dancing, or orienteering.

Week 4 Start increasing your pace, and introduce interval training into your mid-week sessions. Interval training works the body quite hard, so have a rest day afterwards or an easy walk.

Weeks 5–11 Walking at speed means working harder and pushing forwards more. If you have the time, lengthen your midweek walks and ensure that you complete the 32km (20 mile) walk. This is vital, and must be completed two weeks prior to the event.

Week 12 In the last two weeks complete the short fast walks and let your body recover from the 32km (20 mile) walk in time for your big day.

Week	Sunday	Monday
1	4.8km (3 miles) at a comfortable pace (55–60 mins)	Rest 10–15 mins stretch and strengthen
2	6.4km (4 miles) at a comfortable pace (72–80 mins)	Rest 10–15 mins stretch and strengthen
3	8km (5 miles) at a comfortable pace (85–90 mins)	Rest 10–15 mins stretch and strengthen
4	Rest 10–15 mins stretch and strengthen	8km (5 miles) at a comfortable pace (about 85 mins)
5	any other activity for a minimum of 30 mins	8km (5 miles) interval training (about 80 mins)
6	Rest 10–15 mins stretch and strengthen	any other activity for a minimum of 30 mins
7	Rest 10–15 mins stretch and strengthen	9.6km (6 miles) at a faster pace (about 90 mins)
8	22.5km (14 miles) at a faster pace (about 210 mins)	Rest 10–15 mins stretch and strengthen
9	Rest 10–15 mins stretch and strengthen	9.6km (6 miles) at speed (about 78 mins)
10	25.7km (16 miles) at speed (about 208 mins)	Rest 10–15 mins stretch and strengthen
11	32km (20 miles) at speed (about 260 mins)	Rest 10–15 mins stretch and strengthen
12	8km (5 miles) at speed (about 60 mins)	Rest; 10–15 mins stretch and strengthen

Exercise pages • Warming up and cooling down, see Warm-up and cool-down plans p72 • Stretch and strengthen, see Stretch and strengthen plan p73

Tuesday	Wednesday	Thursday	Friday	Saturday	Total km (miles)
4.8km (3 miles) at a comfortable pace (55–60 mins)	Rest 10–15 mins stretch and strengthen	4.8km (3 miles) at a comfortable pace (55–60 mins)	Rest 10–15 mins stretch and strengthen	Rest 10–15 mins stretch and strengthen	14.4km (9 miles)
6.4km (4 miles) at a comfortable pace (72–80 mins)	Rest 10–15 mins stretch and strengthen	6.4km (4 miles) at a comfortable pace (72–75 mins)	Rest 10–15 mins stretch and strengthen	Rest 10–15 mins stretch and strengthen	19.2km (12 miles)
6.4km (4 miles) interval training (about 68 mins)	any other activity for a minimum of 30 mins	6.4km (4 miles) at a comfortable pace (about 68 mins)	Rest 10–15 mins stretch and strengthen	9.6km (6 miles) at a comfortable pace (about 102 mins)	30.4km (19 miles)
any other activity for a minimum of 30 mins	8km (5 miles) interval training (about 85 mins)	any other activity for a minimum of 30 mins	Rest 10–15 mins stretch and strengthen	12.9km (8 miles) at a comfortable pace (about 136 mins)	28.9km (18 miles)
Rest 10–15 mins stretch and strengthen	8km (5 miles) at a faster pace (75–80 mins)	any other activity for a minimum of 30 mins	Rest 10–15 mins stretch and strengthen	16km (10 miles) at a faster pace (about 160 mins)	32km (20 miles)
6.4km (4 miles) at a faster pace (60–64 mins)	any other activity for a minimum of 30 mins	9.6km (6 miles) interval training (about 90 mins)	Rest 10–15 mins stretch and strengthen	19.2km (12 miles) at a faster pace (180–192)	35.2km (22 miles)
any other activity for a minimum of 30 mins	Rest 10–15 mins stretch and strengthen	9.6km (6 miles) interval training (about 90 mins)	any other activity for a minimum of 30 mins	Rest 10–15 mins stretch and strengthen	19.2km (12 miles)
9.6km (6 miles) interval training (90–95 mins)	Rest 10–15 mins stretch and strengthen	9.6km (6 miles) at a faster pace (about 90 mins)	Rest 10–15 mins stretch and strengthen	25.7km (16 miles) at a faster pace (about 240 mins)	67.4km (42 miles)
any other activity for a minimum of 30 mins	11.2km (7 miles) interval training (about 98 mins)	any other activity for a minimum of 30 mins	9.6km (6 miles) at speed (78–84 mins)	Rest 10–15 mins stretch and strengthen	30.4km (19 miles)
any other activity for a minimum of 30 mins	11.2km (7 miles) interval training (90–100 mins)	Rest 10–15 mins stretch and strengthen	11.2km (7 miles) at speed (about 90 mins)	Rest 10–15 mins stretch and strengthen	48km (30 miles)
Rest 10–15 mins stretch and strengthen	8km (5 miles) at speed (about 60 mins)	Rest 10–15 mins stretch and strengthen	8km (5 miles) at speed (about 60 mins)	any other activity for a minimum of 30 mins	48km (30 miles)
4.8km (3 miles) at speed (about 36 mins)	Rest; 10–15 mins stretch and strengthen	4.8km (3 miles) at speed (about 36 mins)	Rest; 10–15 mins stretch and strengthen	Rest; 10–15 mins stretch and strengthen	17.6km (11 miles)

Other pages to help you • Foods for fitness pp90–91 • Preparing for a marathon, see pp106–107 • Any other activity, see pp134–137 • Interval training, see pp110–111 • Using a pedometer, see pp36–37 • Using a heart rate monitor, see pp32–35 • Meeting the challenge pp80–81

WEIGHT LOSS

To lose weight and burn calories you must walk briskly for 45 minutes a minimum of four times a week. How many calories you will burn is dependent on several factors: your age, weight, level of fitness, and how fast and far you actually walk within the time. Your aim is to walk 1.6km (1 mile) in 15–17 minutes.

Use this programme as a guide and adapt it to suit your life. Take into account your weight and fitness to determine which week of the programme you should start at. Your goal is to achieve a good pace and to maintain it for an hour. As you progress, you will find that you are able to walk further in the same amount of time. Start at a pace that is a little faster than your normal pace and increase distance and speed as you feel ready. If your body is not used to exercise it will need a bit of a push each time you walk, but persevere. Try never to miss more than one day of the programme in any given week.

Walking will help you to lose weight, but you need to combine it with a healthy diet to ensure you achieve good and long- lasting results. If you are not used to any physical activity and unsure of your health and ability, please seek medical advice before starting this programme. Invest in a pedometer that states the calories burned, and keep a log. Watching your progress will keep you motivated.

Weeks 1–2 A steady pace means you do not need to push yourself hard, you should aim for 20 minutes per 1.6 km (1 mile). Warm up and cool down for every walk. Try to set aside time for stretching and strengthening. Start with a session of around 10 minutes and extend this as time goes on. Your stretches may be limited to start with, but keep at it and you will soon begin to feel more flexible and supple.

Weeks 3–8 In these weeks you will start to walk further in the same amount of time. At a faster pace you are walking with purpose and should feel that you are exerting yourself, but you should still able to talk as you walk . Introduce another activity you enjoy to your regime, for example swimming or dancing. You have the option to add hill walking in Week 3, which means walking a route that takes you over hills. Hill walking works your body harder and burn more calories.

Week 9–12 Walking at speed means you need to work a bit harder and push forwards a little more. Challenge yourself by following routes that take you over different terrains. By now you could be walking 1.6 km (1 mile) in 14–16 minutes.

Week	Sunday	Monday
1	10 mins at a steady pace	10 mins at a steady pace
2	15 mins at a steady pace	10 mins at a steady pace
3	20 mins at a faster pace	15 mins at a faster pace
4	25 mins at a faster pace	15 mins at a faster pace
5	30 mins at a faster pace	20 mins at a faster pace
6	25 mins at a faster pace	30 mins at a faster pace + any other activity for 30 mins
7	35 mins at a faster pace	20 mins at a faster pace
8	40 mins at a faster pace	30 mins at a faster pace
9	40 mins at speed	45 mins at a at speed
10	45 mins at speed	35 mins at speed
11	35 mins at speed	50 mins at speed + any other activity for 30 mins
12	40 mins at speed	45 mins at speed

Exercise pages • Warming up and cooling down, see Warm-up and cool-down plans p72 • Stretch and strengthen, see Stretching and strengthening plan p73

Tuesday	Wednesday	Thursday	Friday	Saturday	Total minutes
10 mins at a steady pace	10 mins at a steady pace	10 mins at a steady pace	15 mins at a steady pace	10 mins at a steady pace	75 minutes
15 mins at a steady pace + any other activity for 30 mins	10 mins at a steady pace	15 mins at a steady pace	10 mins at a steady pace	15 mins at a steady pace	90 minutes
15 mins at a faster pace	20 mins at a faster pace	15 mins at a faster pace	15 mins at a faster pace	20 mins at a faster pace	120 minutes
20 mins at a faster pace	25 mins at a faster pace	15 mins at a faster pace + any other activity for 20 mins	20 mins at a faster pace	20 mins at a faster pace	140 minutes
25 mins at a faster pace	30 mins at a faster pace	30 mins at a faster pace	25 mins at a faster pace + any other activity for 15-30 mins	30 mins at a faster pace	160 minutes
20 mins at a faster pace	30 mins at a faster pace	20 mins at a faster pace	20 mins at a faster pace	30 mins at a faster pace	175 minutes
35 mins at a faster pace	20 mins at speed + any other activity for 30 mins	35 mins at a faster pace	20 mins hill walking at a faster pace	35 mins at a faster pace	200 minutes
20 mins at a faster pace	40 mins at a faster pace	30 mins at a faster pace	20 mins at a faster pace	20 mins at a faster pace + any other activity for 30 mins	200 minutes
30 mins at speed + any other activity for 30 mins	45 mins at speed	30 mins at speed	45 mins at speed	30 mins at speed	265 minutes
45 mins at speed	35 mins at speed	45 mins at speed + any other activity for 30 mins	35 mins at speed	45 mins at speed	285 minutes
35 mins at speed	35 mins at speed	35 mins at speed	45 mins at speed	50 mins at speed	300 minutes
50 mins at speed	45 mins at speed	50 mins at speed	45 mins at speed + any other activity for 30 mins	60 mins at speed	295 minutes

Other pages to help you • Walking to lose weight pp98–99 • Using a pedometer, see pp36–37 • Using a heart rate monitor, see pp36–37 • Hill walking, see pp112–113 • Any other activity, pp134–137 • Think positive pp78–79 • Posture and breathing pp40–41 • Foods for fitness pp90–91

USEFUL RESOURCES

Australian Podiatry Council
41 Derby Street
Collingwood VIC 3006
Tel: (03) 9416 3111
www.apodc.com.au

Chiropractors' Association of Australia
PO Box 6246
South Penrith
DC NSW 2750
Free call: 1800 075 003
Tel: (02) 4731 8011
Email: nhq@caa.asn.au
www.chiropractors.asn.au
To find a qualified practitioner in your area.

Sissel-Australia
1 Nina Court
Aberfoyle Park
SA 5159
Tel: (08) 8322-9473
Email: sisselaus@telus.net
*For Sissel exercise falls and a variety of top-quality
fitness equipment and health care products.*

New Balance Australia Pty Ltd
47 Wangara Rd
Cheltenham
Victoria 3192
Customer Service Freecall: 1800 654 512
Tel: (03) 9582 5555
Email: info@newbalance.com.au
*For good walk-specific shoes and excellent
measuring service.*

Polar Australia
Pursuit Performance Pty Ltd
ABN 77 946 740 127
309 Pulteney Street
Adelaide 5000
Tel: (08) 8100 8600
Email: polar@pursuit-performance.com.au
For heart-rate monitors and associated products.

Australian Federation of Race Walking Clubs
(NSW Race Walking Club)
1 Hayward Street
Kingsford NSW 2032
Tel: (02) 9349 4862
www.nswracewalkingclub.com

Australian Bushwalking and Camping
Reference Site
www.galactic.net.au/bushwalking
Comprehensive website about bushwalking in Australia.

Orienteering Australia
PO Box 740
Glebe NSW 2037
Tel: (02) 9660 2067
www.orienteering.com.au
*Promotes orienteering events and groups throughout
Australia.*

Confederation of Australia Bushwalking Clubs
(NSW)
PO Box 2090
Sydney NSW 2001
Tel: (02) 9290 2060
www.bushwalking.org.au
Provides lists of bushwalking clubs in Australia.

Walking to school
The following websites provide information and guidance for children and parents.
www.travelsmart.gov.au/schools/schools3.html
www.dpi.wa.gov.au/travelsmart/schools.html
www.iwalktoschool.org

Walk the Walk Worldwide
Mayfair House
4 Christchurch Way
Woking
Surrey GU21 4JU
United Kingdom
Tel: 01483 741430
Email: info@walkthewalk.org
www.walkthewalk.org
For information on power walking, events worldwide and how to join them, and lots more.

International Federation of Aromatherapists
PO Box 786
Templestowe,
VIC 3106
Tel: (03) 9850 9254
Email:info@ifa.org.au
www.ifa.org.au
An organisation especially for Aromatherapists and people interested in aromatherapy. Includes information on courses, events, and where to find a practitioner.

Reflexology Association of Australia Limited
PO Box 366
Cammeray
NSW 2062
Tel: 0500 502 250
www.reflexology.org.au
An independent, non-profit organization. Provides a referral register for people wishing to consult a qualified practitioner.

Australian College of Nutritional and Environmental Medicine
13 Hilton Street
Beaumaris
Victoria 3193
Tel: (03) 9589 6088
Email: mail@acnem.org
www.acnem.org
For details of a qualified practitioner in your area.

International Yoga Teachers Association Inc.
www.iyta.org.au
Provides yoga teacher training and referral services. Contact numbers for the Association are listed in the Yellow Pages phone directory under the heading "Yoga".

Recommended reading
Any cookery books by Jane Sen (Thorsons Ltd, London)
Beautiful books with easy-to-follow recipes and practical advice.

Bean, Anita, *Food for Fitness* (A & C Black Ltd, London; 2002)
A book specifically on sport nutrition.

INDEX

A B

abdomen 52
Achilles tendon stretch 64
affirmations 80
alarm 36
ankle stretch 65, 127
arms 10, 44–45, 46–47
asthma 15
athlete's foot 128
babies, walking with 100
back 14, 32, 52
back stretching 67, 70
backpacks 28, 113
ball crunch 58
ball squats 131
bicep curls 138
black toenails 130
blisters 128
blood pressure 15
body awareness 120–21
body-scanning 120–21
Borg scale 32–34
bottled water 85
breathing 40–41, 76–77
bridge 57
Brothers, Dr Joyce 133
bum bags 28, 29, 116

C

calves 52, 65, 71
carbohydrates 90, 91
carbonated water 85
charity 103, 104–5
children 102–3
chiropodist 19
chlorine 85
city walking 39
clothes 24–27, 113
coffee 87
cooling down 68, 72, 121
core muscles 33, 52

corpse pose 71
country walking 39
cross-training 121, 134–36
cycling 134

D E

Da Vinci, Leonardo 17
dancing 134–35
darkness 116, 117
dehydration 84
depression 15
diaphragm 76
diet 98
double leg stretch 54
dreams 80–81
endorphins 15
exercise 13, 15, 32, 34, 76
exercises 137–39
    see also strengthening
    exercises; stretching

F G H

fats 86
feet:
    massaging 119, 123, 124–25
    size 19, 22
    walking and 42–43
    width 19, 22
filtered water 85
fingers, swollen 130
fitness 32–35
flexibility 32
foods, healthy 86–87, 90–91, 99
footprint analysis 18
fruit/vegetable portions 87, 88
gastrocnemius muscles 52
glycogen 90, 91
Gore-tex shoes 113
gym, training in 136–39
half marathon 148–49
hamstrings 32, 65

"happy hormones" 15
heart 32
heart rate 11, 34, 35
heart-rate monitors 34, 35
heel-to-toe rock 129
heels: slim 19
hiking boots 23
hills 109, 112
hip flexor stretch 64

I J L M

ingrown toenails 130
injuries 126–31
interval training 36, 111
Iyengar, B K 75
juicing 89
Lao Tzu 31
legs 42–43, 46–47
logs 98, 120, 158–59
lower body stretches 64–65
lunges 137
mantras 82
marathons 81, 84, 90–91, 103,
    107, 150, 160
Martial 119
meat 86
meditation 82
mind 13, 15, 76, 78, 81, 82
mineral water 85
minerals 88
mistakes 48–49
Moonwalk 105, 160

N O

neck stretch 60
negativity 78
oestrogens 85
omega-3 fatty acids 86, 87
organic food 88
orienteering 103
osteoporosis 14, 135

overseas events 105
overtraining 121, 136
overweight 13
oxygenated water 85

P Q R
pedicure 119, 122–23
pedometers 28, 29, 36
plantar fasciitis 130
podiatrist 19
positive thinking 78
posture 40–41, 48–49, 120, 137
power walking 10
benefits of 9, 11, 13–15
technique 42–47
pregnancy 100–1
premenstrual tension 15
pronation 18, 19
protein 90
purified water 85
quad stretch 127
racewalking 11, 106–7
rain 24
raised cat stretch 101
resources 154–55
rest days 121
road walking 111
rollerblading 135
routes 38–39, 95, 96
rucksacks 28, 113
running tracks 38

S
safety 116–17
salsa 134
sand 113
school, walking to 102
Sen, Jane 86, 88
shin splints 126, 129
shoes:
    buying 20
    caring for 22–23

lacing 22–23
    qualities of 21
trail walking 113
tread wear 18
walking and 20–23, 121
wet 23
shoulder stand 77
shoulder stretch 62
side rolls 66
single leg stretch 55
sleep 15
socks 27, 121
speed 34
speed walking 10–11
sponsorship 104–5
sports bras 26
sprains 126–28, 129
spring water 85
sternocleidomastoid muscle 52
strains 126–28, 129
strength 32
strengthening exercises 51, 52,
    73, 121, 128
stress 15
stretching 51–55, 52, 60–67,
    68–73, 73, 121, 127, 128
strides 36–37
strolling 10
sunglasses 29
sunscreen 29
supination 19
swimming 134
Swiss balls 56–59, 131

T U V
tap water 85
teenagers 103
Thoreau, Henry 109
thought 78
toenails 130
toes: size 19
trail walking 112–13

treadmills 111, 136-37
tree, the 69
tricep dips 9
tricep stretch 61
Twain, Mark 9
upper back stretch 63
visualizations 81
vitamins 88–89

W Y
Walk the Walk 6, 104–105, 160
walking:
    ability 38–39
    adjusting 42–43
    advanced 144–45
    beginners 140–41
    as cardiovascular aerobic
        activity 11, 13–14
    categories 10–11
    companions 95, 96–97,
        113, 117
    competitive 106–7
    events 103
    fitting in 94–95
    ill-health, prevention of 14
    intermediate 142–43
    short distance 146–47
    styles 18
    time for 94–95
    weights and 45
    see also power walking
walking groups 95, 96–97
warming up 68, 72, 121
water 84–85, 91
water bottles 28, 29, 45
weight loss 98–99, 111, 152–53
weights 45
wind 24
yoga 69, 71, 77

WALKING LOG

You will find that you make fast progress with power walking in every way: physically, mentally, and emotionally. There is always something to learn from each walk, not just about your pace and how far you could walk, but also about how you felt. Use the comments column in this log to record your thoughts so that you can keep track of the training weeks you really enjoyed and those that you didn't, how hard or easy you found each walk, whether you felt any aches or pains when you were stretching, and so on. The weather, seasonal changes, family life, even landscapes all make a difference to your attitude, how you feel, and how you perform on the day. Photocopy this page to keep your own monthly record of your progress.

Month No:

Date	Distance	Time	Calories /Heart Rate	Route	Comments

Date	Distance	Time	Calories /Heart Rate	Route	Comments

ACKNOWLEDGMENTS

Author's acknowledgments

This book has been created with the help and support of some very special people. I want to thank my partner, Guy, who modelled his walking skills and supported me with patience and a smile, for which I cannot thank him enough; my family, for always believing in me; Sonia Doherty, for her Chiropractic skills and knowledge: Jane Sen for her wonderful attitude towards food; Nigel Fisher, for his help with podiatry and chiropody; Cathy Orpin, for advice on Pilates; and to Clare Maxwell-Hudson, for her advice and encouragement.

I would also like to thank the team at DK, in particular my editors, Jennifer Lane and Jenny Jones, for their infinite patience and care, which I truly tested; Mary-Clare Jerram for recognizing just how important it was to have a book on power walking; and finally to all my gorgeous, loving friends who are always there for me!

A percentage of the royalties from this book will be donated to Walk the Walk Worldwide for breast cancer research and holistic cancer care.

Publisher's acknowledgments

Dorling Kindersley would like to thank photographer Russell Sadur and his assistant, Nina Duncan; models Guy Aubertin, Heidi Baillargeon, Lisa Rachel Bautista, Nikol Johnson, Cherie Greer, Amy Sobieraj and Jennifer Lane; Sharon Weems for photoshoot production and location services in Miami; clothes stylist Liz Hancock; Naomi @ Code Management for hair and makeup, and Peter Rea for the index. Special thanks to Jo Lee at Reebok UK (www.reebok.co.uk) and Lynsey Mailer at Cake for all trainers provided; Leanne at USA Pro for sports clothing (www.usapro.co.uk), and www.heartratemonitor.co.uk for the heart-rate monitor.

Picture credits

The publisher would like to thank the following for their kind permission to reproduce their photographs: 102: Masterfile UK/Ariel Skelley; 103: James Abelson; 104 and 105: Guy Aubertin; 106: Empics Ltd. Illustrations by Phil Wilson. All other images © DK Images

About the author

Nina Barough has always been intrigued by the relationship and balance between mind and body. She has been a vegetarian from a young age, and studied massage and reiki. She finds power walking a wonderful way of achieving this balance while maintaining her passion for good health and fitness. For many years, she ran her own successful fashion styling and production company

In 1996 her life changed when she had the idea of power walking The New York City Marathon wearing a customized bra in order to raise money for breast cancer research. The idea became a reality and the charity Walk the Walk was born.

Only months later, Nina was diagnosed with breast cancer and her holistic attitude towards healthcare played a vital part in her approach to her treatment and recovery process. Walk the Walk Worldwide follows Nina's philosophy of life by raising money for breast cancer research and holistic cancer care and by encouraging people to take responsibility for their own health and well-being.

Nina continues to lead groups of power walkers in marathons and walking challenges around the world, helping to raise millions of pounds for her charity.